Krishna Prem in 2021.

You are born a buddha. You die enlightened.
This book is about who you are from three years old when you lost your innocence until nine months before you leave your body when you regain your innocence. In other words, what happened to you for the better part of your life while you were completely unconscious.

When you are in the womb, everything is provided for you. Love, food, and security surround you. Birth is a wake-up call. Immediately you realize there is no turning back. You take off like a rocket ship in search of yourself. Your life is the future. You simply don't have time for the present. Instead of being real, you develop a personality to protect yourself.

You get a job, a wife, two and a half kids. Your buddha nature simply can't keep up with your dreams, and chases after you from behind. Your buddha nature can't be shaken, but as you do not have eyes on the back of your head, you can't see him. Until, that is, you hit the wall.

At this point, you crash and burn. In meditation, this wall is called the dark night of the soul. You now have two choices. You can bounce off the wall and return to your old tired life. Or you can see the buddha now in front of you and try to join him.

If you go back to the old, you will be welcomed back by your family and your conditioning with open arms.

After all, misery loves company.

(continued on back page)

Aloneness

A Love Story

by

Michael Mogul

(Krishna Prem)

Aloneness, A Love Story

Michael Mogul (Krishna Prem)

Library of Congress Cataloging-in-Publication Data

Copyright © 2021 by Michael Mogul (Krishna Prem)

All rights reserved.

All Osho quotes copyright Osho International Foundation www.osho.com

No part of this book may be reproduced in any form or by any electronic or mechanical means including information storage and retrieval systems, without permission in writing from the author. The only exception is by a reviewer, who may quote short excerpts in a review.

Printed in the United States of America First Printing: August 2021

ISBN 978-1-63068-187-6

Contents

Introduction 1

Chapter One: Rejoicing in Your Aloneness 3

Chapter Two: Life is the Balance 17

Chapter Three: Your Only Wealth 32

Chapter Four: Be Grateful to All 44

Chapter Five: Love Plus Meditation 61

Chapter Six: Drown Yourself 75

Chapter Seven: Radiate Love 87

Chapter Eight: Love Plus Meditation 100

Chapter Nine: Be an Individual 118

Chapter Ten: You Have Come Home 130

Chapter Eleven: Absolute Freedom 142

Chapter Twelve: Inner Emptiness 155

Chapter Thirteen: Witnessing is Your Secret Love 167

Chapter Fourteen: Sound and Silence 179

Chapter Fifteen: Watch Your Thoughts 191

Chapter Sixteen: Don't Worry, Be Happy 206

Introduction

Celebrate aloneness, celebrate your pure space, and a great song will arise in your heart. And it will be a song of awareness, it will be a song of meditation. It will be a song of a lone bird calling in the distance – not calling to somebody in particular, but just calling because the heart is full and wants to call, because the cloud is full and wants to rain, because the flower is full and the petals open and the fragrance is released...unaddressed. Let your aloneness become a dance. Osho

This little book was created and written from March 2020 over the course of a year of social distancing. I think you may well agree that the subject of aloneness came up for all of us during this pandemic. Many of you could write a book called loneliness. I have added a touch of self-love and awareness to my life and fell in love with my aloneness...the twin sister of loneliness. To be honest, it has not been an easy relationship. Thus, I insist that you challenge everything I write to find out what is right for you. Enjoy. Krishna Prem

I left Boston 48 years ago and walked all the way to Bombay. I cannot walk on water, but I paced up and down the aisles of many a Boeing 747. I was 27 years old and my life was falling apart.

Astrology friends called this my Saturn Return. I called it my nervous breakdown.

I ended up at the feet of my friend Osho. Osho asked me "What kind of meditation do you prefer?" I didn't really know what "meditation" meant, so I just said, "I love to walk."

Osho laughed and said, "Walking is a great meditation. Your arms are moving one way, your legs are moving the other way, and if you are alert you will end up in your *hara*, which is the home of meditation."

With this in mind, I invite you to take a walk with me. Reading my book, you'll find yourself moving one way, then the other way, then all over the place. With luck, you'll find yourself becoming centered.

Oh, by the way, if you find a few roses among the stories, don't forget to stop and smell their fragrance. Osho always reminded us that the journey is the goal.

Chapter One

REJOICING IN YOUR ALONENESS

Rejoicing in your own aloneness is what meditation is all about. The meditator is one who dives deep into one's aloneness, knowing that we are born alone, we will be dying alone, and deep down we are living alone. So why not experience what this aloneness is? It is our very nature, our very being. Osho

Speaking about myself, it took me forever to be in touch with my aloneness. Loneliness made me fearful. I wanted to cling to somebody, to some relationship, in order not to feel lonely.

Deep down I knew I was in pain. It took me years of meditation to have the courage to confront myself, to become friends with myself. Now I can be your friend without being needy. I can walk beside you in my own shoes. Join me. Krishna Prem

Out of your loneliness, you have invited everybody in the world to live with you. And your life is just one big crowd. Take a step back from yourself and see who you've brought along: parents, relatives, girlfriends and boyfriends, colleagues at work, social pals, teammates, teachers, bosses, employees…not to mention the virtual hordes following you on Facebook, Twitter and the rest.

They define who you are. They are you, molded as a reflection in their image. And as you've already noticed, this book is called *Aloneness, A Love Story* — a title that's not going to hit the top spot on the New York Times Bestseller List any time soon.

Why not? No, it's not just my lousy writing. It's because the book that you and everybody else have been reading for eternity is titled *Togetherness, a Love Story*. It takes two to tango, right? In other words, longing for a soul mate, finding true love, bonding with friends…this is the opium dream of our collective mind because it means we need never feel our loneliness.

Most of the movies we see conclude with, "…and they lived happily ever after." The reason they say that, as we all know perfectly well, is because we want to believe that love is forever. And what we want, Hollywood is happy to provide because that's what fills the till at the box office.

Karl Marx was wrong. Religion is not the opium of the people: Hollywood is. But then, Tinsel Town hadn't been invented in Marx's day, so the old, woolly-bearded thinker can be forgiven. He died in 1883. He didn't even get to see one of those early, black-and-white, Mickey Mouse-loves-Minnie Mouse cartoons in the late 1920s.

In my first book, *Gee, You Are You*, I shared colorful stories about my life. My new book, *Aloneness, A Love Story*, is about my spiritual life where I am talking about meditation. But then why, you may ask, is the title referring to aloneness? Well, because really I have no choice. If I want to talk about meditation I have to address the uncomfortable issue of aloneness.

That's where Osho comes in — he's an expert on both. I'll tell you more about this later, but let me start by recalling how Osho said to me, "You need to clean your basement, Krishna Prem."

When I first met him, I said, "Osho, I didn't have parents, I didn't have a family life. I was brought up by a sister. My life is so dysfunctional, I am so glad you are saying we can just move straight ahead to meditation."

He replied, "Who said that? If you are not healthy and you meditate, it will not work. Unfortunately, in your case, I have a lot of work to do, because we need to start on your primary issues. So that when you meditate, you don't bring your past unfinished. You can't go from a dysfunctional life into meditation, you need to heal first."

That was my invitation to drop the past. I got the point; only when you drop the past can you learn to meditate. First, I cleaned my basement. Now I am in the attic. I am meditating and cleaning the attic.

Osho told me, "Once you do that, you can go into your living room and relax. Once you are again comfortable in your own skin, sitting in your favorite chair, having a beer, listening to music, then you can be a happy, healthy human being."

By the way, I'm not trying to recreate Osho by writing this book — trust me, he's got plenty of books of his own. I am trying to explain the context in which we can become happy, healthy human beings, based on my own experience.

So, once you finish your housecleaning and once you learn to meditate, you can start living in your living room. Osho said to me, "It is amazing but most people, instead of cleaning the basement, instead of learning how to meditate, instead of learning to relax in their living room, remain standing outside on their own porch and never come in."

We are outsiders when we could be insiders. We are strangers in a strange neighborhood. Nobody is living inside themselves. Nobody is wondering, *Who am I?* Everybody is saying, "I will tell you who I am, once I am rich enough, or famous enough, or successful enough, not to be in pain."

It does not happen like that. Rich people are in pain wanting to be happy and poor people are in pain wanting to be rich. We need to participate in our own lives but we don't

know how. You need to find the door of your own house, open it, leave the porch behind and enter inside the home of your being...oh, yes, and you're welcome to have a beer in the living room.

This book is all about looking at life from inside the house, looking from the state of meditation out into the world. And the person reading this book, nine out of ten times, is doing just the opposite: looking from the outside world at meditation. I've got news for you; meditation is not a spectator sport. You can't look at it. You can only be it.

We are going to look at what trust looks like from the inside out.

We are going to look at what love looks like from the inside out.

One of the keys in this book is to ask yourself what you want, and it's unlikely to be a static answer, because what you want is an ever-shifting target. It's an ongoing journey. Even when you know what you want, you are still going to have to follow a steep learning curve, mastering the art of not falling asleep when you reach a comfortable plateau, look around, stretch, yawn, and start to think, *Hey, this is good enough. Let's chill.*

Many people learn just enough so they can live their lives on a seemingly snug and secure plateau. But it is never that way. There is always another moment to climb and grow. When you stop growing you begin to die.

The real winner again and again is a meditator who loves life, who enjoys himself while at the same time finding inner fulfillment. Someone who understands how to add meditation to daily life.

I am glad to be alive. I am glad I am participating in my own life and, in the words of Walt Whitman, doing my best to "celebrate myself." Participation is often hard work, but sometimes it can be music, song and dance.

Now, if you do not happen to be a fully conscious, fully awake human being — and let's face it, they don't arrive on Planet Earth by the busload — you are going to do many things wrong. Life is often going to tear you up, but if you have passion, you are going to look forward to it. If you don't have passion, it's going to be hard work, but if you add passion to work it becomes a play.

Passion is not created by your parents. It is created by you. Oftentimes, the passion that your parents wanted to instill in you was experienced as pain. Your parents of course, meant well, but mostly they were busy, anxious, stressed-out people who never really had the time to stop and meet you — the real you.

Did your parents ever say to you, "Time to go to your piano lesson? Time to go to dance class?" Or perhaps they said, "You don't play well enough, you're wasting your time." Many people give up because they are told they are not good enough and, in a way, it is true.

You don't just walk up to a piano and become an instant Mozart; you have to put in the time and the effort, but you also have to ask yourself, *Is it worth it? Is this what I love?*

If it is really coming from you, Mozart is not far away. If it is coming from your parents, Mozart is somewhere a couple of light years beyond Uranus — no crudity intended.

The role of parenting is to give space and love. If you offer just space, there is no shape to it. If you offer love as well as space, the child can grow, can make mistakes, and is big enough to become himself or herself.

Talking of space and love, people who are in love can swing both ways, if you don't mind me giving a novel twist to a popular sexual expression. They offer so much love it stifles you, or they demand so much space you begin to wonder why there's no love in the room. For me, it is both, it is love and space together.

You may have noticed by now that I'm not comfortable with linear, rational, step-by- step thinking and a steady progression in concept development. It's not my style. My thinking is all over the place. In fact, sometimes I don't think at all. But if you take my hand and come with me into this book, I promise you I'll take you to a place of profound understanding and deep insight where you will say, "I got it. Thank you, Krishna Prem."

You don't need to be an over-educated intellectual to make this journey with me. In fact, that could be a handicap. Which reminds me, my heart goes out to all those young men and women who in these troubled times of COVID-19 are graduating from college and university and can't find a job because the global economy also caught the virus and is in intensive care, being intubated.

Going through all that disciplined thinking and learning, just to be unemployable? To misquote Bob Dylan's "Subterranean Homesick Blues," after twenty years of schooling there's no day shift to get on. I mean, it takes quite a sense of humor to appreciate the cosmic joke when the coronavirus just stole your future.

But, joking or not, the current education situation offers a lesson to be learned; when they toss their black mortarboard caps into the air on graduation day, in which direction are these ambitious young people looking? Of course, to the future, to their careers, to the challenges and successes that lie ahead of them.

But where does life happen? Not in the glittering mirage of the future. It happens here, now, in the present moment. It requires no degrees, no graduation. It demands no success, nor failure. It's happening whether we bother to recognize it or not.

So, a stolen future doesn't have to be a disappointment. It can be a blessing, an opportunity to live in the only place where anyone can ever live. In one, single, ungrammatical word: "herenow."

One of the reasons people don't meditate is because they don't understand the concept of being in the moment. When I say, "Be here, now," they don't get it and neither did I for a very long time until I pierced the question.

Here, in the present moment, time does not exist. Theoretically, like Stephen Hawking, Carl Sagan, and other popular scientists have patiently explained to us, time exists as a continuum: flowing from the past, through the present and into future.

In reality, this flow is just an appearance. It appears in the mind, because the mind has the ability to recall the past and think about the future. Beyond this shadowy realm of mental construction, neither past nor future exist. No, really. Trust me. They don't. There is only now...now...now....

"Excuse me, Krishna Prem, what time is it?"

"Now."

"Are you shitting me?"

One of the big concepts in this book is: be here now. Sure, you can schedule your life, make appointments, pretend that time exists — everyone else is pretending, too, so it's convenient to tag along.

Time is mind. I forgot who said that, maybe Albert Einstein, but anyway it's true. Past/present/future are crammed into your mind, together with all the stress and pressure that time, or lack of it, creates in you. When you think about it, it's truly bizarre: first we invent time, then we complain there's not enough of it.

Like the White Rabbit said, as he glanced at his watch while hurrying past Alice, "Oh dear! Oh dear! I shall be too late!" Chances are he got so stressed he developed a stomach ulcer and died of a heart attack.

One can't help conjecturing that he'd have been better off getting totally ripped with a hookah-smoking caterpillar. Grace Slick and Jefferson Airplane could have shown him the way

— insider's joke for those of you old enough to remember the 1960s.

But I digress. Here's the bottom line: this whole book is about how to get your mind to work for you, instead of your mind being your boss, stressing you out and creating stomach ulcers.

People don't meditate, because they don't know about the concept of being in the moment. Eckhart Tolle keeps telling them to appreciate the "power of now" but somehow they don't hear him. They actually think the past is their life — can you imagine?

We don't need to deny the past. We need to become friends with the past. We need to thank our past for teaching us enough to bring us to the point where we can kick the past in the butt, preferably over a cliff, and then take a jump into the present.

What I want to do in this book is show people how the past can become a teacher. So that when you look into the past, you can say "Thank you, fuck you…and fuck off!"

Once the burden of the past disappears and you can live in the present, you can shrug off the emotional weight you've been carrying all these years. When you can really be in the present, this moment feels so brand new to you, that you know it can't possibly be a continuation of something old.

You find yourself saying "What is my situation this morning? How can I make my life work for me? How can I be creative? How can I respond freshly, innocently, immediately to this moment that's opening up in front of me?"

You forgive your ex-wife and thank her for teaching you what love is, by teaching you what love is not. Then there is a possibility not to simply meet somebody new, but to do things differently next time instead of repeating your old mistakes, entering into a new adventure.

People ask me what I am still doing in India after 48 years. What is wrong with me? And what is wrong with me is that I love Osho. I think he is a genius. Beyond being enlightened, I simply love what he put together and what he did for me — or rather, what I allowed myself to do to myself with his guidance, encouragement, and support.

I will never forget that feeling, the first time I did Kundalini Meditation — one of his inventions. I cried aloud, "Oh, my God! How did I not create this meditation myself?" It was so simple, four stages lasting a total of one hour: shake for fifteen minutes, dance for fifteen minutes, stand or sit for fifteen minutes listening to music, and then lie down and become enlightened again, every day.

I want to suggest something to you: get out your old CD, or your old audio cassette tape if you are as old as me, and try the Kundalini Meditation again. Or, if you don't have it, or have never tried it, look it up on Spotify. I will share the link.

You can be at home, turn on Spotify, press Kundalini, and have the shake of your life. This meditation brings me into the moment. I call this meditation "getting divorced" because when my wife was with me and I was about to begin Kundalini Meditation, I would mentally grant myself a legal separation from my significant other. When you meditate, you can't bring anyone with you. In my imagination, I whispered in her ear, *Guess what? You are not with me right now. Our relationship is over. Finished.*

Then I would shake, dance, sit and meditate. And then I would go out looking for my wife, looking forward to seeing her, because I'd become a brand-new person, involved in a brand-new relationship.

For me, the shaking is dropping the past, dropping my marriage, dropping my parents, being alone and as the result of being alone, you might find that you enjoy your wife, you enjoy your parents, you enjoy your friends. So funny: you need to get divorced to find your wife again.

Many people think that, when they have completed Kundalini Meditation, they have meditated for one hour. Strictly speaking, that's not true. Yes, you've done the technique for an hour, but the shaking is not meditation, the dancing is not meditation, the sitting and listening to music is not meditation. It is all preparation for that final stage, when you finally take the risk: *I* am alone. I am lying here, on my back, eyes closed, doing nothing and it feels okay. I feel brand new in my life right now. I feel relaxed.

For those previous 45 minutes you were preparing yourself to slip into the present moment. It may feel a little weird to lie down and do nothing, neither active nor sleepily passive, neither speaking nor snoring. Just think: Zen monks do this all the time, so fifteen minutes isn't going to kill you.

Give it a try. Take a risk, take your clothes off, take your parents off, take your beloved off, be alone and see what comes out of it, or, more accurately, into it. It is brilliant. It is called life. Enjoy!

Krishna Prem here. Congrats on laboring through my first chapter. This fool loves company. If you want to know more about me for FREE, go to my website www.geeyouareyou.com and click on Book. The first 50+ pages of my first book Gee yoU aRe yoU about me and how I met my teacher and friend Osho open up magically on your computer screen, no need to print them. Or go directly with this QR Code:

If you want to know more about yourself, practice the Osho Kundalini Meditation for 21 days. The music is free on Spotify. Go to www.spotify.com and search for Osho Kundalini Meditation. Or go directly to Spotify with this QR Code:

Instructions for Osho's Kundalini Meditation can be found on www.osho.com. In fact, all of Osho's active meditations can be found there, including Osho Dynamic Meditation. Yahoo!

Please consider learning more about the Hooponopono technique. YouTube is your best bet. I especially respect Dr. Hew Len on YouTube.

Reading is one thing. Reading as meditation is another. To help you lose your mind and enter into the world of no-mind, I have created a YouTube channel called "Aloneness A Love Story" with over 50 meditations for you to play with. I strongly suggest you choose one meditation from my YouTube Channel after you read a chapter. It will help you turn your everyday "maditation" into meditation.

I cannot promise that you will become enlightened by being with me, but I can help you lighten up! For example, go to www.youtube.com and go to my channel, "Aloneness A Love Story," and search for The Numbers Game by yours truly. Or use this QR Code:

Here is the QR code for all 50+ meditations:

On my channel, you will bump into the best meditation teachers in the world. Krishnananda and Amana, Miten and Premal, Sudheer, Shunyo, Tarika, and Rupa as well as Satyarthi and Anubuddha, to name a few of my good friends. And soon to be good friends of yours as well.

Of course, I need to give a shout-out to my brother Dr. Brian Alman, because if I don't, he will disown me. Brian is a mountain peak of hypnosis. When I went east 48 years ago to meet Osho, Brian went west to live with Dr. Milton Erickson, the father of modern hypnosis. Brian gave me many private hypnosis sessions. And I shared Osho Dynamic Meditation with him. I once asked Brian how is that we could scream during Dynamic Meditation in one moment and dance in another. He laughed and suggested that anger and ecstasy are neighbors in our minds. And he suggested what Dr. Erickson shared with him; when in doubt, go deeper!

Brian's QR code is:

Chapter Two

LIFE IS THE BALANCE

Sadness gives depth. Happiness gives height. Sadness gives roots. Happiness gives branches. Happiness is like a tree going into the sky, and sadness is like the roots going down into the womb of the earth. Both are needed, and the higher a tree goes, the deeper it goes, simultaneously. The bigger the tree, the bigger will be its roots. In fact, it is always in proportion. That's its balance. Osho

I am a human being and, on the other side of life, I am a human doer. When these two guys play together, I consider this to be a successful life. To be only one of them, for me, is not a successful life. I like the idea of both.

There is one very cute story about Osho that illustrates how he was so much into just being, not doing. He was wearing a Rolex watch that was given to him as a present and he didn't like that watch because it stopped all the time.

Rolex watches are built to have perpetual motion, so for people who like to run up and down hills all day, a Rolex works perfectly, but the problem was that, although in his younger days he loved to go running, especially in the very early morning, Osho didn't run anymore. He was just sitting in his chair all the time, not moving, so the watch stopped.

Osho said, "I don't like this watch." So, we then committed Rolex sacrilege. We took out the guts of his expensive Rolex and replaced them with the guts of a cheap Timex worth no more than ten dollars. The watch was no longer run by perpetual motion, it was run by an ordinary battery, but it ran all the time, whether the guy who was wearing it moved or not.

Osho then said, "Well, I love this watch now. It always works!"

Sometime later, it must have been shortly before Osho left his body — as the saying goes — we created some fancy new pyramid buildings in the Pune resort, but we didn't have enough money to install the air conditioning, which in India is absolutely essential.

Osho was a practical man. He said, "Sell these watches and with the money put in the air conditioning."

I should mention he had lots of fancy watches, not just one Rolex. We didn't know Osho was about to leave his body, because he kept it a secret, so we just thought he was being practical.

Later on, after Osho's departure, the woman who bought the Rolex called me and said, "I made a donation for a Rolex and it has the guts of a Timex. It's not worth anything!"

We promptly said, "Oh please, don't be nervous. We kept the guts of the Rolex and we are going to send them to you as a present, so you can put them back in."

Still, she was very upset until she found out that actually it was Osho who had wanted to install the Timex clockwork.

One of his favorite expressions was, "I am a simple man, I like only the best."

Well, he wanted the best watch, but it didn't work on his wrist, so we had put something cheap and fake inside his expensive Rolex. It's a cute story and reflects how busy we normally are, always running around doing, whereas Osho was just the opposite.

Meanwhile, I have been meditating on the idea that life is oneness and out of this oneness comes you and me. But somehow we don't really get this, so we live in denial and in separation. We live in duality.

For me, life is orgasmic and out of this universal orgasm, men and women are created. Of course, there's the minor practical detail of how exactly we are created, through biology and sexual orgasms, but I'm talking about the big picture and the big orgasm.

Life is oneness and out of it we create duality in multiple forms, such as religions like Hinduism and Islam, and such as politics like Democrats and Republicans. In other words, life is one, and it is the mind and language that create division. Before mind and language do their thing, there is nothingness and there is silence, and in that silence there is aloneness.

This truth has been ripped away from us by parents, by religion, and by the school system. In other words, silence does not make money. Silence is not useful. Silence does not require you to fall in love with the other, but it is not loneliness.

I want to say to all my friends who are reading this book that you probably think I am crazy because I consider meditation more important than the marketplace. But I think you are crazy if you think the marketplace is more important than meditation. So somehow, we are all crazy.

The idea of this book is that I can share my madness with your madness, because separation is an illusion and really there is no distinction, so I am not talking about you *or* me, I am talking about you *and* me. For me, the most important word in the English language is the word *and*. Not you *or* me. But you *and* me.

Meditation is only one percent of the truth. What you are doing today in the world is the other 99 percent. The problem is that the world is always focused on the 99 percent. For example, you have a car, you have a home, you have a wife, you have a child, you have a mortgage...this is what makes up the 99 percent.

Then one fine day, when you go inside yourself, you discover meditation, the missing one percent. So, the world is saying, "Who cares about one percent when you already have 99 percent?" In terms of mathematics and economics, this attitude makes sense.

However, this book is really about the idea that the one percent is more valuable than the other 99 percent. Even though it looks like an imbalance, when it comes to meditation that one percent is crucial because it is basically who you are, while the other 99 percent is who you have been told you are.

The reason why I am writing this book is because even though I spent 48 years in India focusing on the one percent and asking myself who I am, I am not satisfied with it. It does not really turn me on. What turns me on is adding that one percent to the other 99 percent because then I find I am 100 percent myself.

Water boils at 100 degrees Celsius. If you run the water out of your tap, fill your kettle and switch it on, you can easily bring it to 99 degrees. But if it does not boil, it remains just hot water, which is what it is, until you add that extra one percent. That one degree that makes all the difference…water immediately turns into steam and your personal kettle starts hissing, whistling, singing, and filling your whole kitchen with music.

Like I say, the most important word in any language is the word *and*. Because what is more important to us: one percent or 99 percent? We don't know who we are. You may be rich and famous but you don't know who you are unless you add that one percent to your 99.

By the way, I don't want people to finish reading this book and buy a ticket to India to spend 48 years there like I did. I don't want that to happen. I am so happy I came home with my one percent and met you with the other 99 percent.

You looked at me like I am onto something and I looked at you like you are onto something. And the truth of the matter is, we are both onto something. It is not me or you, it is me *and* you. So, add me to your life, I will add you to my life and then we are home, we are turning from water into steam and singing and whistling.

I am in love with the symbol of infinity. It is like a number eight on its side. Nobody knows exactly where it came from but most probably, like most things, it came from the Ancient Greeks, who probably got it from somebody else.

Anyway, that's not why I love it. I love my own symbolism that I put in the symbol. On one side of the eight, we have you as existence, the one percent. On the other side we have you as the marketplace, the 99 percent. In the center of the symbol there is a dot where the lines cross.

How do you add that one percent, let's call it consciousness, to the capitalistic 99 percent? How do you get those two guys to like each other? The only way, for me, is to breathe into that dot that separates enlightenment from the marketplace. Meditation and the marketplace are separated by a dot.

The concept that I live with is: this dot is another name for your ego, which includes everything your parents, your politicians, and everyone else has been telling you about who and what you are. For most people, nearly all people, the 99 percent is really important and you think it's all you need for this lifetime, so you can provide for your wife, your children, and get along comfortably in society.

Now there are a few people like Jesus, Buddha, or Osho, who have said that the one percent is the only thing that is valuable. For them, that one percent is enough. They felt so rich with their inner riches, they lost interest in any kind of outer riches.

But I often question the people who think they love Jesus, Buddha, or Osho, while at the same time focusing their attention exclusively on their 99 percent. To me, that 99 percent is not worth anything unless you can move into the other side of the infinity symbol, where you can experience the same degree of self-love as those guys did.

Then, when you say, "I love you, Jesus," there is no separation between you and Jesus. Anyway, Jesus of Nazareth was just the outer form of a man who discovered his own inner Christ consciousness. So don't fall in love with people, fall in love with who they really are, because they are also Christ consciousness and that's why they are so much bigger than the person you think they are.

A regular guy in the world who is living up to his 99 percent level, is always going to think of Jesus as a guy with a long beard and olive skin, who walked on water, healed the sick, never made love, and didn't care about money. A regular guy with an ordinary mind is creating that fantasy, just like millions of people are doing around the world. In fact, he is telling Jesus who he is, while never asking, "Who am I?" and from that perspective meeting Jesus.

Jesus would never say "Be Jesus." He would say, "Be your own Christ consciousness in your own person. Use me to fall in love with yourself. Then we can have a great time together. But don't abuse me by adoring me and praying. Find out who you are."

So, I went to India for 48 years and you spent the same 48 years paying your mortgage and raising a family. You think you need a break, maybe even go on a meditation retreat, but what we all really need is to get rid of that dot. That dot is the ego that is separating meditation from the marketplace.

How to get rid of it? My feeling is the solution lies in our breathing. Breathe into that dot. Everybody in the world thinks that the dot is solid and you can't get through it. I say the more you breathe into that dot with the question "Who am I?", the more expansive the dot becomes.

It becomes bigger and bigger, and when solid things become bigger you can literally see holes in them. You can see there is way to meditate and also to be in the marketplace. All of a sudden, there is no such thing as separation.

When you breathe in and you breathe out, when you watch your breath, the ego becomes bigger, which may seem strange at first because all the mystics say this is what we need to get rid of in order to experience oneness.

Some of us go to India and the master looks at us and says, "Drop the ego, just drop it." "But how can I drop my ego if it is not real?" I ask.

When you breathe into the dot, you find that ego is not real. When you breathe into it, you experience space and awareness and gradually you discover you can combine your one percent with the 99 percent.

So, it is about breathing. I have to breathe into meditation in order to see that I love the marketplace and I'm asking my friends who are in the world, reading this book, to breathe in the other direction: breathe into the marketplace in order to see that you love meditation.

I am asking: breathe into your dot to allow that one percent that does not know who he is or she is, and give it a chance to play with the other 99 percent. Breathing in and breathing out this way, you may not drop the ego but you may find that it is not real. The more real you become, the less real your ego will become and you begin to experience the real person in you.

In other words, breathing is very important: not just in a physical way, to keep your body supplied with oxygen, but also in spiritual way, to embrace yourself in your totality.

Osho, for example, would always breathe out. He was not concerned about the marketplace. He didn't give a shit about his body, or about money, or about what the world thought about him, he only breathed out.

When I am worried about my rent, I am only breathing in. So, in that moment I am in the 99 percent, breathing in so I can pay the rent and support my family. And, like I say, most people only breathe in and never breathe out.

In my way of looking at life, a successful person knows how to breathe in and breathe out. I breathe in when I need to take care of myself and then I breathe out to remember that I am the witness, the consciousness behind the mind, behind every experience that I have. So, then I can look at my life in a bigger way.

How can you be big enough to make the marketplace a meditation, instead of an ongoing problem of survival? Just breathe. When you breathe in and you breathe out, life begins to look really good.

You can do it yourself for a few minutes right now, as you read my book. Just breathe in and you find you arrive at a place where you cannot breathe in anymore and you begin to breathe out. Then you will find a place where you can't breathe out anymore and you breathe in. In these two places, where the breath pauses between in and out, this is the place to watch the gap.

The cosmic vision that I see in the infinity symbol is that you breathe in as a human doing, focusing on the marketplace, and breathe out as a human being focused on meditation. Both need you, and you need both in order to breathe in and breathe out.

My gut feeling is that the human being and the human doer are in this together and not really separated by the ego we talked about. They are actually in a state of oneness and this is what we are looking for in this book: the oneness in life which makes it wonderful.

I will never forget when a spiritual seeker, almost crying, came to Osho and declared,

"Life is awful."

He chuckled and said, "That is amazing. You see that life is full of awe!"

I want you to stop polishing your personality and polish your window instead. Polish your window so that you can look at existence through a clear window. In fact, with meditation, you don't have to clean that window, you need to open that window, you need to fly out the window and become one with this existence that you think is outside yourself.

Love yourself. Realize there are more than seven billion windows on this planet but only one sky, and this sky is mirroring the ocean. The ocean is one. The sky is one. The sky and the ocean are in oneness.

So, one way is to go down to the bottom of the ocean and see how many waves are up there on the surface. And the other technique is to rise up into the sky, look down and see how many people are looking at the sky through their own window.

When you polish your window without opening it, you are just rewriting your personal story so that it works, so you can handle life as it changes and shifts, so your personality gets more and more rich.

This book is asking you to stop with your stories and ask yourself, "Who am I?" And then when you fly out through your window, you will still have a story, but that story will be a dance with oneness. Everybody will see that your window has opened and you are out: your eyes are shiny, you can't tell anybody anything, but they will see you are out and now you can be with someone in a whole new way.

That is what Tantra is: you are in the sky, she is in the sky, and you are flying together. You are in the ocean, she is in the ocean, and you are swimming together, two waves just smiling at each other.

So instead of polishing your ego, instead of being content with your old story, let it be a brand-new story. Your story, up to now, has not been rooted in reality. It is just a compilation of what everybody has been telling you, which you took upon yourself, and which worked fine for society. And what will work well for society, is just a fragment of the real you.

Find out what you want to do as an individual, so you can enjoy and embrace your own creativity. Don't look back to the past and say, "I am going to duplicate that." Rather, look at the present and say, "Hey. This is new and interesting. I am going to enjoy this!"

By being in this moment, you may even fuck up, but at least you will be brand new, at least you will be energetic, at least you will be dancing. At least you will be one with the universe instead of one with the United States.

When you are one with the universe, you can even vote if you like, so I'm not saying you need to drop out, but you will see that the most important thing is who you are, in this moment, and not the guy who is asking you to vote for him.

By the way, there are downsides to meditation. For example, you will discover that you cannot put your faith in politicians anymore, but you will vote anyway and enjoy the dance. And when you go to church you will find you don't believe a word the priest is saying, but you will really enjoy singing.

In fact, as you begin to meditate more, there is a chance you are going to remember how much fun it is to sing...in the shower, in the church, along with the car radio.

It only takes a few minutes to write a song about the five happiest moments of your life. If I ask you to write a song about misery, it would take forever. I don't want to do that to you, because you will end up thinking you are miserable, which isn't who you are.

Next time you take a shower, I want you to remember a happy moment in your life and sing a song about it. From then on, every time you take a shower, you can think of a happy memory, sing a new song, and see if your voice gets better and you get more courageous.

Then life becomes an opportunity to sing a new song whenever you can think of five new moments that are making you happy. It seems to me that singing in the shower actually helps people get in touch with their inner light. It wouldn't surprise me if some people have gotten enlightened in the shower.

Actually, a better technique for getting close to enlightenment is soaking in a bathtub. There is a moment in the bathtub where you can let go completely and just relax. Then you can receive whatever existence wants to tell you.

The way I heard it, Albert Einstein was feeling frustrated because he knew he was close to discovering the Theory of Relativity but it lay just beyond his grasp. Then one day, he got into his bathtub, let go of all his mental tension and the truth appeared in front of him.

Did you ever hear that? Maybe it is not true. But for sure he liked to spend lots of time in the bath, pondering over the universe and its workings.

By the way, speaking of Einstein, can you list three original thoughts that came from you? Is not your mind really just a storehouse of thoughts you borrowed from everybody else…from the media, the history books, the internet, the opinion-makers and the rap singers?

The challenge is realizing that you are a robot. The challenge is realizing that everything you do has been pre-programmed by your parents and the social system they represent. You are just a product of your environment, instead of a product of who you really are, given by existence.

We are looking for balance here, so please don't kill yourself because you found out you are a robot. Let the robot go to work tomorrow as usual. Don't take it seriously, after all, you have been the robot for so long, it is pretty easy to fake it. So relax, go to work and nobody will ever know that you are looking into your own life.

No one could know, no one's even going to guess. Not even one percent of the world is meditating and the other 99 percent will not even think about it. You can actually have fun with playing as your robot at work, but please don't tell anybody that you are watching yourself. Don't tell anybody you are seeing yourself as the doer. Don't tell anybody that you are meditating. It is a very personal thing that has nothing to do with anybody else.

To watch yourself work, to watch yourself talking to people and playing at being a normal robot, will bring you so much joy. You may feel clumsy at first, because your habitual behavior programs will start breaking down as soon as you start watching yourself. But you'll soon get the hang of it.

So just watch yourself and start breathing into it. I can guarantee your life will not change nearly as much as you feared, but it will add a new dimension of delight. And believe it or not, there will be a few people in your life, who, after a while, will recognize you are laughing about the same things you used to cry about.

There will be one or two people who might confess to you, "I am also becoming the witness, I am also watching myself in the marketplace, I am also watching the noise of the world that's somehow turned into a symphony orchestra. It is amazing how much I thought my life was just noise. Now I am finding out that I am an orchestra leader."

Enjoy the music but don't tell anybody, just be yourself. And let's see if anybody picks up on it. I think it will improve your love life; I think you might get a raise at work. People will want to know, "How is it that you see the big picture and I can only see my problems?" But don't go around bragging. There's no need. Just go around living your own life.

Chapter Three

YOUR ONLY WEALTH

Remember, only that which you can take with you when you leave the body is important. That means, except meditation, nothing is important. Except awareness, nothing is important, because only awareness cannot be taken away by death. Everything else will be snatched away, because everything else comes from without. Only awareness wells up within. That cannot be taken away. And the shadows of awareness - compassion, love - they cannot be taken away. They are intrinsic parts of awareness. You will be taking with you only whatsoever awareness you have attained. That is your only real wealth. Osho

We all identify with how we look. Do we look good? Do we look bad? Are we overweight? Am I attractive? That is all very normal and understandable. In fact, the truth is, we know more about our outer body and how it looks than anything else.

But what this book is about, is coming from who you really are. So, my feeling is that we also have an inner body, and an inner weight, and an inner beauty. But they are undernourished, because we haven't been breathing in and breathing out.

When we breathe in, when we are taking care of a physical play, we are breathing in life, we want to feel good, we want to look good. But here's the thing: when you think about it, you don't want to look good just because somebody else pays you a compliment. That's nice, but it also makes you completely dependent on someone else's opinion.

Really, you want to look good because you actually feel good. So, I want you to be aware that you have an inner body and an inner weight. And this is what makes life interesting, because since we have gotten into fashion, skinny people have taken over, the models weigh about ten pounds each and in order to even think about becoming a model today, you have to be really, really thin.

Then, as people rebel against this ridiculous norm, there is a tendency to swing to the opposite polarity and the models get really, really big. And this is what life tends to be about. It is so extreme, either the model weighs ten pounds and she is beautiful, or she is popular because she weighs six hundred pounds and she is ugly. I'm exaggerating, of course, but there's truth in what I'm saying.

I say there is a big territory in the middle called, "How much does your inner body weigh?" You are also in a body that does not have shape, or weight. When you start to meditate, you start to ask yourself, *How do I feel from the inside out?*

Our whole life is about how do I feel from the outside in, and many of us just don't feel so good about ourselves. When you don't feel good about yourself, you are actually saying no to meditation and no to your inner body.

So, I want you to look at who you are not, which means that ultimately you are not this physical body that you walk around in. Because the revolutionary thought in this book is that existence does not have a body. I'm sure many of you know the old Zen koan, "Find out your original face, the one you had before you were born." In other words, do you know how you looked before your parents made love?

You have always been here, your soul has always been here. Let's say, right now, for example, you are your inner nothingness manifesting in physical appearance as a woman in Spain. I am my inner nothingness appearing as a man in Amsterdam. So how do you get from being nothing to be that woman in Spain? It seems so unbelievable.

And the funny thing is, when you say this to yourself, that this is so unbelievable, you are actually saying, "I am unbelievable." Maybe you don't want to listen to me because you're in the middle of a wonderful love story with a guy who thinks you are the most wonderful woman in the world. And maybe you are worried whether, one day, when you get older, he will still love you.

This is exactly how meditation can help, because meditation is the understanding, "Yes, I look good and, yes, I'm identified with my attractiveness because I love the way this guy is passionately kissing me, but we are also going to grow into love." Being physically beautiful is not nearly as important as being a person in love.

So, what I'm saying is that you have an inner body, which in terms of spacetime location lies somewhere between how you look in the big picture, as existence, and how you look in the mirror, as a person. The problem is that in the middle exists your emotional body, and unless you meditate, your emotional body just does not feel worthy enough to be relaxed, comfortable and happy. It does not feel good.

If you can get to a point where you can look at what I am saying, you may not get it the first time, you may not get it the last time, but the thing I want you to realize is that you are existence appearing as a woman, existence appearing as a man.

When you understand that, you just naturally get better looking. When you look out at the world around you, at the people around you, your eyes begin to shine.

One funny example I can share with you is that, when I went to India, my spiritual teacher asked me to wear an orange robe and a necklace of wooden beads with a picture of him hanging from it. In India, these things are called "malas" and just about everybody has some kind of mala, even if it's hidden in a box at the bottom of their wardrobe. That meant that I was his "sannyasin" or disciple.

After a few years with Osho, coming and going, we were having trouble getting into the country because the Indian authorities didn't want our kind of meditation to happen, so they would often give us trouble at the border.

Osho, who is a very pragmatic kind of spiritual teacher, then said to us, "Instead of getting in trouble, just wear street clothes and get rid of those beads and orange robes. Those were a good awareness technique, but now you don't need them anymore."

But then he added, "The only problem is that you look good and your eyes are shining. You have been humbled by existence and you look really good, so they may guess you are one of my sannyasins anyway. And I can't do anything about that.

"Most people are not prepared to see how beautiful you are, so most of them will not see your shining eyes and your open heart, but it is a risk that we are taking. Those who pay attention, they will notice. But that is the best I can do for you. Just take off all those things that make you look like you are a meditator, and just walk through life, giggling at all the people that don't know their uniqueness."

Meanwhile, let's go back to the infinity symbol, which, as you recall, looks like the figure eight on its side. On one side you are a "somebody" with a physical body who is concerned about the way he or she looks. On the other side you are a "nobody" and the cuteness of being nobody is that you get in touch with the feeling of being one with existence. And many of the mystics in India say that once you become a nobody, everybody lives inside of you, which means that basically you own the whole universe.

However, you are in Spain right now and when you meditate, the whole country of Spain lives in you. Could you be richer? How can you be lonely when everybody lives in you? In other words, you are as big as existence. You can actually witness the whole existence when you are a nobody. I personally think this is a great thing.

But, if I may give you a gentle reminder, it is actually not such a great thing until you are okay with paying the rent for the house you live in. In other words, for me to know that I am existence is only half of the experience. I also need to be able to pay the rent. But once you know how big you are, paying the rent is not the biggest thing that has ever happened to you.

Meditation does not necessarily give you the money to pay the rent, and that is what is fun. You need to also create a person who can do both, so the idea of this book really is, again, how to be one with existence *and* pay your rent, how to be one with existence *and* be in love with another foolish human being, how to be one with existence *and* feel okay having two children and a mortgage.

It does not pay the bills but it does give you a space from which to watch. This book is about watching. Once you can witness life, you can see the ins and outs and laugh at the story.

For example, I like a story that happened to me a while back, when I went into Starbucks one fine day, somewhere in Southern California.

The waitress asked me, "How are you doing today?"

I said, "Gosh, I am having such a good day! I am about to give a talk on meditation. I am leading what I call a meditation workshop and it is going to be full, so I feel complete and excited."

She answered, "Wow, that is so good that you are enlightened and that will be $6.25 for your café latte and almond croissant."

In other words, you still have to pay your breakfast. She really was a Zen master for me in that moment, because she basically said, "Guess what, I am glad you are happy, and you also need to pay for what you just ate and drank."

So, when you read my book, I wouldn't want you to get so high that you go to Starbucks and walk out without paying for your coffee. That would be not a great idea and might get you in a lot of trouble. We don't want the fact that you are a meditator to create a situation that might put you in jail, we want you to get out of the jail you are already in.

Jail is for me is when you don't ask yourself who you are, when you ask somebody else who you are. As soon as somebody tells you who you are, you are in jail. So don't listen to anyone else.

Even if they say you're looking good — compliments are always nice, right? — make sure this resonates with how you feel in your inner body. And by the way, you might not need as much coffee in future, because once you start listening to yourself, you begin to get a lot more energy without a caffeine hit — or any other kind of hit, come to think of it.

To be honest, coffee is my only drug now as I get older, but I use it as a crutch. I don't have enough of my own energy and I still need to espresso myself. I need to be exciting, I need energy to brush my teeth, and sometimes I can't brush my teeth without a cup of coffee — if I am not feeling good about myself.

So, the key is to check when you feel good about yourself, then you begin to let go of drugs. We only take drugs to feel good and eventually they become a crutch. You know how it goes; you need more and more drugs to reach the same great experience you had yesterday.

So my answer, again, is to breathe. Just breathe in to be the doer and breathe out to be the guy you know you really are. When these two become one, you will get the energy from it. This is my feeling, so this is where I want to take people.

Now here is a beautiful story about my friend Veda Prem. After I left India in 1975, I opened a meditation center for Osho in California. I had no money, so people had to pay to work there.

Everybody had to pay $300 to live, eat and work. Geetam was the name of the place and it was in the Lucerne Valley, in the high desert, about two hours' drive from East Los Angeles.

Anyway, back in 1975, $300 was a nice piece of change and Veda had a hard time getting it together. Finally, he had the money and got a ride to Geetam with a friend. They were driving a convertible and they both had $300 each.

On the trip, Veda was reading a book and he used the $300 as a bookmark when he got tired of reading and tossed the book on the back seat. At one point there was a gust of wind and the $300 flew out of the car and he didn't even notice until it was way too late to go back and look for it.

Upon his arrival, Veda says to me, "Krishna, I don't have any money, what can I do?" And I said, "Veda, I love you, but you can't live here without paying."

He was very emotional about it and I felt terrible. But there was nothing I could do because we were just getting started and all of us were close to broke.

So I said, "Veda, there is only one solution. There is a woman here, she is blind and she wants to go to India to meet Osho. She is willing for me to choose a friend of mine as her guide." In other words, I would pick the person who would go with her to India.

So out of this situation, which at first looked miserable for Veda, he got a plane ticket to India with all expenses paid for one month. The woman was very thankful because he was really a good caretaker as well as a beautiful man and he took his responsibility as her caretaker very seriously.

The blind woman had an amazing month, then flew back to the States, but Veda decided to stay on and spent the next five years in Osho's ashram in Pune.

Five full years, with no money, not even a penny. He was welcomed as a member of the commune surrounding Osho, so he was given food and shelter. Whenever I was there, he thanked me so much, because it turned out to be a miracle in his life.

In the commune, everyone was given a job and so Veda was asked to do shopping for vegetables. This was important, because the ashram was vegetarian, so there was no meat, not even chicken and fish — which, by the way, some Californians consider to be almost vegetarian. But we weren't vegan — I don't think the word had even been invented in those days — so we did eat eggs and dairy.

Well, dairy…in India…that was a no-brainer because you can't live in India and not consume milk products. For one thing, the main sustaining force in the nation's daily nutrition intake is chai, which is tea boiled with spices and milk and…oh my god…don't forget the sugar. Lots and lots of sugar. Mostly, it's not a question of having sugar with your chai, but having chai with your sugar. Super-sweet chai…an amazing experience enjoyed by over a billion Indians.

Also, as a meat substitute, Indian cuisine contains a lot of paneer, which is a kind of cottage cheese, looking and feeling rather like tofu. Palak paneer, shahi paneer, mutter paneer...lots of India's favorite dishes are loaded with it.

Anyway, Veda's job was to get up early every morning, around 5:00 am, and go to Shivaji Market, a few kilometers away, and buy vegetables. He had to be first at the market to pick out the best veggies, because he was selecting them for Osho's meals.

It was still dark and he couldn't use the light on his iPhone because Steve Jobs hadn't yet invented it, so he'd bring along a small flashlight to survey the veggie stalls. He made most of his choices by feeling and smelling.

Veda became a kind of celebrity at Shivaji Market, because he was a very blond guy, with pale skin and blue eyes, totally unlike all the locals, who, without exception, had dark hair, brown eyes, and a permanent suntan.

The stall holders loved him, especially because he never checked the weight of the goods he purchased, so they could all rip him off a little bit every morning and make a few extra rupees. Everyone in India knows Westerners are loaded, right? So, it's only fair to charge them extra.

I don't know if it's true, but I heard a rumor that Krishna who, in the Hindu religion, is considered to be the perfect incarnation of God, said he'd be coming back next time as a blond, so they totally loved Veda. He made two trips to the market every morning: the first for Osho's supply of veggies and then a second, bigger trip, to buy veggies for the rest of us.

Veda spent five years at the ashram, then another four-and-a-half on the Rajneesh Ranch in Oregon, where — get this — he ended up wearing a soldier's uniform, peaked cap and all, guarding Osho and wielding a semi-automatic Uzi rifle. I swear to god it's true, because I saw him myself, on guard duty, standing near the podium where Osho gave his daily discourses.

Now that's what I call taking care! The veggie shopper had mutated into an armed guard. I guess it was necessary, because you know how trigger-happy Americans are. When they don't like people, they don't just write a letter to the editor of the local paper, they declare war and re-enact the gunfight at the OK Corral. And they certainly didn't like Osho.

Veda didn't shoot anybody, though, so for him it was a karma-free experience. Jeez, the things we did with Osho! By the way, the Ranch managers never gave me an Uzi to carry. I guess they didn't trust me.

Veda stayed with Osho all the way through until he left his body in January 1990. Then Veda went to live on the East Coast of the States and soon found a job taking care of super- wealthy stockbrokers in their grand Long Island mansions. As you can see by now, he was an excellent caretaker and even the hedge-fund kings of Wall Street could appreciate it.

So, you could say that he worked for free for Osho, but when it came to anyone else he required a fat salary. Half-jokingly, his employers would say to him, "Well, you did it free for Osho, why am I paying you so much? What's the diff?"

And he would say, "Because I love Osho with all my heart, whereas I care for you as a job. In fact, I want a Christmas bonus."

It is a beautiful story. I have often seen how people who did well in Pune, taking care of Osho and the community, were afterwards successful in the world.

In Pune, once you got the knack of meditation through practicing techniques like Dynamic Meditation and Kundalini Meditation, you joined the commune and work became your meditation. It was a love affair and Osho would often say that work is love made visible. In my friend Veda's case, it was absolutely true.

It makes you wonder: what if those $300 hadn't blown away out of the back seat of the convertible, on his way to Geetam? Or if he hadn't been reading that book? Maybe none of this would have happened. Or it might have happened in a way that was not as rewarding for him. Sometimes we think we are being cursed with bad luck and it turns out to be the best thing that ever happened to us.

One moment you're in the California desert, shedding tears because you can't stay in a meditation center the way you'd planned. Next moment, you are shopping at five o'clock in the morning in India and feeling like you just won the Euromillions Lottery Jackpot.

Osho got the right food and Veda also got the right food. As a matter of fact, so did I. Love plus awareness is meditation. Spiritual food.

Chapter Four

BE GRATEFUL TO ALL

Be grateful to everyone, because everybody is creating a space for you to be transformed – even those who think they are obstructing you, even those whom you think are enemies. Your friends, your enemies, good people and bad people, favorable circumstances, unfavorable circumstances – all together they are creating the context in which you can be transformed and become a buddha. Be grateful to all. To those who have helped, to those who have hindered, to those who have been indifferent. Be grateful to all, because all together they are creating the context in which buddhas are born, in which you can become a buddha.
Osho

So, here we are: 36 years on from the destruction of Osho's big commune in Oregon, and I'm surprised to see that Netflix still finds the subject interesting enough to release a documentary titled *Searching for Sheela*.

It's about the life and times of Sheela Silverman, aka Ma Anand Sheela, the Indian woman who became Osho's secretary in 1981 when he decided to leave his ashram in Pune and travel to America. Sheela was put in charge of building Rajneeshpuram, our spiritual commune for 3,000 people, on a disused cattle ranch in Central Oregon.

The Netflix documentary begins in present times, tracking Osho's publicity-seeking former secretary as she leaves her home in Switzerland to make a celebrity tour of India. Her visit took place in late 2019, just before the coronavirus pandemic shut down the world.

But this Netflix documentary turns out to be a piece of fluff. It has no guts. Sheela glides from one TV talk show to another, from one dinner party to the next, hosted by admiring members of Delhi's social elite.

The interviewers don't give her a hard time. She denies trying to murder anyone and nobody hammers home the point that, back in 1986, she pleaded guilty to such crimes and received a 20-year prison sentence.

Okay, let's allow ourselves to be blind as well as generous and forgive Sheela for

trying to reshape her past. Nevertheless, it's a one-woman personal campaign that's unlikely to succeed. Too much awkward history gets in the way.

"After 35 years people are still talking about it," she complains to one of her hosts in the documentary. Well, Sheela, maybe that's because the actual facts never seem to mesh with your fantasies.

But let me back up. This documentary about Sheela would never have been conceived if it hadn't been for the wildly successful Netflix six-part series *Wild Wild Country*, released in 2018.

It documented the arrival of Osho in Oregon during the long hot summer of 1981, showing how hundreds of his red-clad sannyasins arrived soon afterwards, swiftly building a township for themselves in order to live with him.

It also tracked the escalating conflict between "the Rajneesh" – as we were called – and the local ranchers, the religious fundamentalists, the State of Oregon and, last but by no means least, the Reagan Administration in Washington, DC.

While working on another movie project in Oregon, the film makers had discovered a treasure trove of old videotapes of Sheela and other people involved in the conflict. They hit on the idea of showing these video clips as flashbacks, while interviewing the same people as they are now, more than thirty years on. It was a winning formula and became a global success.

Osho was not the star of *Wild Wild Country*. Osho was in the background, while Sheela was at the forefront, along with local residents, government officials…oh yes, and lots and lots of lawyers.

So, it was Sheela versus everybody else in the whole world and Osho was not given any screen time by Netflix to convey his message. Basically, it was a political thriller – a good documentary but not deep enough to include Osho's approach to meditation. As entertainment, it got a "10" from me but as a meaningful insight into his work, it scored a lamentable "0."

To say that Sheela faced a difficult challenge in establishing a community of red-clad aliens in the middle of Marlboro Country is a massive understatement. We were from Mars, they were from Uranus — a planet whose name sounds suspiciously like "you're an asshole."

We were meditators from the Mystic East, they were fossils from the Old West. In fact, one of the nearest towns to the Ranch was actually called Fossil. We wore red, but, hey, they were the rednecks.

By the way, I suspect it was never meant to be peaceful relationship. Osho was simply too provocative. His ever-growing collection of Rolls-Royce s and his support for our takeover of the nearby town of Antelope were enough to alienate 99 percent of Oregonians...and it only got worse from there.

My feeling at the time was that Osho wanted Sheela to get under people's skin and her sound bites on the local television news channels did just that. She called everyone who was against us "bigoted, biased, and prejudiced" or, more simply, "a jerk." As the conflict grew, so did her terminology, graduating from "bigoted" to "fucking bigoted" and similar phrases.

People still ask me, "Krishna Prem, you've been with Osho for 48 years, how come I didn't see you in the Netflix documentary?" The answer is pretty simple. Sheela and I hated each other. Most of you have heard of the "law of attraction" as a way of manifesting what you want in life. Well, I used to call Sheela the "law of unattraction" as a way of describing why I and many others didn't want her in our lives.

It wasn't just that Sheela didn't like me. I had the same feeling towards her. From the beginning, it was not a match made in heaven, so I was never put in front of a television camera and asked to talk about Osho, Sheela, or the Ranch.

In the previous chapter I mentioned how, in 1975, I bought a 70-acre property in the Lucerne Valley, Southern California, and turned it into an Osho center with the name Geetam.

Well, the first time I ever spoke to Sheela, she was calling me from India. I was running Geetam and, at that precise moment, was as happy as a pig in shit because a wealthy American who'd fallen in love with the place had just given me a large donation.

Alas, Sheela got to hear about it and called me to say, "The center of Bhagwan's work is in Pune and the center is not strong enough. Please send the check to India."

I nearly cried. I nearly died. Well, as I recall, I did cry. Because, you know, running that center was an expensive business, and the donation had just made my life very easy.

But at the same time, I had to acknowledge the truth in her message. Pune was the epicenter of Osho's earthquake. It was the sun in our spiritual galaxy, around which little planets like Geetam orbited. I sent the check to India. I cried and cried.

But good fortune prevailed and I was able to buy Geetam and keep it flourishing, even without that fat little check. Which reminds me: shortly before buying Geetam I wanted to show Osho what it looked like, and in those days we had no mobile phones to take pictures and I didn't even have a decent camera.

So, I sent Osho a glossy brochure of the ranch that I was buying. It was a dude ranch for girls in high school who would go there to learn how to ride horses and spend a weekend bonding with their new, four-legged friends. It was a nice brochure, showing pretty girls riding horses, and it also showed off the property.

And I asked him, "Osho, do you like the idea of turning this into a meditation center?" He immediately answered "Yes" and as a loving gesture sent me a statue of a rooster. That was such a cute gift. It was made of silver, and the wings, body, and face moved independently.

It was a fighting cock, and that made me laugh because I guessed it was an implicit message from Osho that it was going to be a fight to keep Geetam afloat, which certainly proved to be the case.

It was my habit in those early days to spend nine months running Geetam and three months living and working at the ashram in Pune. Once Geetam got going, it attracted many Americans, especially Californians, and I recall sitting in front of Osho one night, in Pune, when he asked me, "Krishna Prem, how come so many people are coming to me through you?"

And I said, "I'm in love with you." That was my answer. Here, I must say to the reader, that's not who I am anymore. These days, I'm more about awareness than love. So, I couldn't say that now, but back then, I was so in love with Osho that I was a magnet to people who were also seeking this kind of connection with an enlightened mystic. They could feel him through me.

When I was spending time in Pune, I was treated like any other worker in the ashram. I did a variety of jobs and it must have been in the winter season of 1980-81 that I was given the task of planting more trees around Buddha Hall, which was where Osho gave his daily morning discourses to a gathering of hundreds of sannyasins.

It was hard manual work and at the end of each day I felt absolutely exhausted. It so happened that, during this tree-planting time, I was one of the very few sannyasins who was told that Osho would soon be traveling to America. I was sworn to secrecy, so I couldn't even tell my girlfriend, but it gave me a great idea how I might be able to sneak out of tree planting.

I sent a personal note to Osho asking, "Do I really have to plant trees if we're not going to be here forever?"

He sent the message back, "You're not tree planting trees for you. You are planting trees for the trees."

I had a good laugh because at that moment I was really puffing up my ego, knowing I was one of the few people who knew about Osho's travel plans. I figured that trees were redundant in an ashram that was about to be abandoned – they just didn't matter.

But I was wrong. Osho was saying to me, "Get off your ego trip. I'm going to America, but you still need to plant those trees with love."

At the end of my stay in Pune, I went back to Geetam and, sure enough, a few weeks later, it was announced that for medical reasons Osho had left India and come to America. He arrived in New Jersey in June 1981, and meanwhile Sheela was scrambling to find a property in the US big enough to build the "new commune" that Osho was envisioning for his disciples.

I was hoping he would choose Geetam, but it wasn't nearly big enough. Instead, as I've already mentioned, Sheela bought a 120-square-mile cattle ranch in Central Oregon, on the dry side of the Cascade Mountains.

Immediately, sannyasins were arriving there to start the huge building project, but meanwhile Osho's therapists and group leaders were all leaving Pune. They couldn't wait for the Ranch to be built. They needed an already-existing facility where they could continue to offer workshops and trainings, thereby generating urgently needed cash for the Oregon commune. So Osho sent all the therapists to Geetam and it became his new "Multiversity."

Multiversity is a cute word. Instead of the usual term university – "uni" meaning "one" – it was all about diversity. It was a great idea and a great name, very catchy. But the problem for the little guy now writing this story was that Geetam was suddenly way too important for me to be allowed to continue to run it. I had to make way for others.

From one day to the next, I went from being President and Founding Father of Geetam to dishwasher. And I really got a kick out of that, too, because Osho said I could continue to live there, even though the new administration considered me to be excess baggage. They didn't really want me around because as an ex-boss I knew more than they did. Anyway, that's how I became the chief bottle-washer and dishwasher at the place I started.

About eight months later I was asked to come to the Rajneesh Ranch and this was seen as a feather in my cap, an honor to be invited, because there were thousands of sannyasins around the world longing to travel to Oregon. But the shortage of accommodation and restrictive land use laws meant only a few hundred of us could live there permanently – at least in the early days.

But boy, work on the Ranch was difficult. Look at it this way: I consider myself to be an interesting person. I can run an Osho center, raise money, take care of hundreds of people. I can wash dishes. But that's pretty much the limit of my abilities.

To tell the truth, I'm not the best person in the world for doing anything practical.

More than anything else, I like to look cool, hang out, drink coffee, and talk to pretty women. And the problem was that the Ranch was all about functional, practical construction, with nuts and bolts, hammers and nails, timber and concrete. It was based on doing...doing...doing. Really, I wasn't a great asset to have around.

But then I was given an unusual job. Sheela badly needed Americans to come to the Ranch because the majority of Osho's sannyasins were Europeans, especially Germans and Italians, closely followed by Australians, Brazilians and Japanese. The only thing that was missing was Americans.

So, Sheela gave me a room in Rajneeshpuram's cozy, comfortable, newly-built hotel and gave me a phone connection with no bills to pay. She said, "I need you to call all the Americans who have visited Geetam over the years and invite them to come and live on the Ranch."

She needed Americans for a variety of reasons, but mainly it was because they could be legal residents and vote in the local and state elections.

I thought this was a great idea, more suited to my modest abilities than planting trees or building houses. So, I moved into the hotel, got on the phone and started calling everybody who had ever visited Geetam.

There had been hundreds of people moving through our center in the Lucerne Valley and I had a record of all their addresses and phone numbers. So, I was pretty confident I could persuade them to come to Rajneeshpuram, thereby making an important contribution to the creation of our new city.

However, I soon discovered there was a major snag. Whoever I contacted and invited invariably said the same thing: "I don't want to live with Sheela."

By now, Sheela was all over the American news networks, insulting everyone in sight, using four-letter words and generally being absolutely impossible. So, I could understand their reluctance to come under her control.

Then I hit on a feasible approach. I said to them, "Look, I'm not inviting you to come and live with Sheela. I'm inviting you to come and live with Osho." At this, most of them would begin to relax and consider the idea, and then I'd follow up with, "Just come for a week, feel it out, and see if you want to live here."

I didn't say we need you to because you are American. I didn't say we need you to vote. I just said, "Come for a week and see if it's you."

Many of them still hesitated and said, "I'm not sure. I feel confused." I bring this up because, while talking with them and trying to persuade them in a light-hearted way, I'd say things like, "Hey, I know how you feel. I feel the same way about living with Sheela, yet I was pulled here by Osho. I don't know what I'd do in your place. It kinda makes me discombobulated."

Let me explain to my European and Asian readers that "discombobulated" is a fun American expression for saying, "I feel confused." I was able to sympathize with these people because deep down I wasn't happy at the Ranch. The work had been killing me. The only thing that wasn't killing me was living in a nice hotel room making phone calls.

Naturally, every few days, I'd have to report to Sheela and tell her how my project was going. I'd tell her how many Americans I'd invited and I also explained to her my strategy of inviting them to come for a short stay to feel out the Ranch and see Osho again.

Then, one time when I was talking with Sheela about my progress, she said, "Okay, but I'd like to be alone now. I'm actually very tired. I feel discombobulated."

And I remember thinking to myself, *Wow, that's amazing. I just used that word myself, today. Is she psychic? Is she enlightened?*

It wasn't until years later that I found out that my hotel room had been wiretapped. So, she'd heard me tell my friends "Hey, I wouldn't want to live with Sheela either! The only reason I'm here is because I want to live with Osho."

So, as you can imagine, in retrospect, I was pretty high on Sheela's shit list, although not, I'm happy to say, on her hit list. She never tried to rub me out.

After a while, when I'd exhausted my contacts, I was transferred to driving buses. Our Ranch fleet consisted of yellow, secondhand school buses that we used to ferry people around the Ranch, and we ended up buying so many of them that we became the second largest public transit system in Oregon, right next to the City of Portland.

Now you're talking about a job I can do. I loved driving buses. It was stress-free. All I had to do was pick people up, drive around the Ranch, drop people off. No worries. No problems with Sheela or her lieutenants. I worked the same 12-hour shifts as before, when the work was killing me, but now, with this job, I loved it.

When work is fun, I call it play. When work is difficult, I call it work. Well, I was playing now. I was having a great time. And I was very busy driving those buses.

One day, I got a message that Sheela wanted to see me as soon as possible. As it turned out, "as soon as possible" took a very long time, because life without Sheela in my face felt so good that I just never seemed to have the time to go to "Jesus Grove," as her trailer compound was called, and shoot the breeze with her.

Like I said, we were working 12 hours a day, seven days a week, and although I might have easily managed to make time for a date with one of my lovely female passengers, I just never got around to talking to Sheela.

Then, one fine day, my bus was flagged down by one of Sheela's lieutenants — some self-important guy with his own pickup truck, wearing jeans and a cowboy hat, with a Motorola slung around his hip as if it was a Colt 45. He was a little bully enjoying his power, whom I disliked just as much as I disliked Sheela.

He said to me, "Krishna Prem, how come you haven't been to see Sheela yet?"

I shrugged and replied, "Well, she gave me the message to come as soon as I could and I've just been too busy. I thought, if it's important, she would come and see me, you know?"

Sheela's lieutenant just hated that answer. I mean, he was pissed. He stuck out his hand and said, "Give me the keys to the bus. You're fired. We want you to leave the Ranch right now."

I couldn't believe it. I couldn't figure out what I'd done. Like I said before, I had no idea she'd been tapping my phone and listening to my sympathetic "I also hate Sheela" calls to my contacts.

So, I gave him the keys and got off the bus. I'll never forget that moment because I had to walk back to the townhouse where I was staying. I didn't have a vehicle anymore. I was walking home to pick up my stuff and leave the Ranch. And suddenly I realized that I wasn't sad about it. I wasn't crying. I was actually relieved.

As I was walking, there was a friendly "beep beep" behind me and a sleek 4x4 Ford cruised up and offered me a ride. The driver was a beautiful American woman called Sunshine, out of Seattle, Washington, who, like many of my friends, was totally in love with the Ranch and with Osho. She worked in the PR department and press liaison. All the visiting male journalists adored her sassy, sexy style.

She powered down the window and asked, "Krishna, what are you doing walking home in the middle of the day?"

And I said, "I've just been kicked off the Ranch."

She gave me a ride, then asked me what had just happened. I replied, "I really don't know. I think it's because I'm not the kind of guy you would hire to build a city. You might hire me to run a city, but you wouldn't hire me to build it."

Sunny was upset that Sheela had given me the boot.

"I would never leave the Ranch just because that bitch told me to," she commented. But Sunny had protection, because she had a special connection with Osho and it would have been difficult for Sheela to get rid of her, whereas with me it was easy.

But there was another difference, too. Like I said, I felt relieved. I was actually happy to leave the Ranch. So, I don't want this tale to indicate that Sheela was absolutely wrong about everything. Somewhere, I think she was right to ask me to leave, because I just wasn't a gung-ho cheer leader for commune life.

But then again, looking back, I might also say to Sheela, "You weren't really Ranch material either, because in the end you fucked up."

Sheela used to say she wasn't interested in meditation. She liked the world, she liked the marketplace, she enjoyed the feeling of power and she liked kicking ass. That was okay with me, but it doesn't work for too long around mystics like Osho, because

57

sooner or later you discover that you need both qualities: meditation *and* the marketplace.

If you want one but not the other, it's not going to work. So, you can say that Sheela was simply a worker, and it didn't work. I was simply a meditator, and it didn't work. What works is a balance of meditating and working. So I don't blame Sheela as much as you think I'm blaming her. It was a Catch 22 situation in which maybe everyone was pushed into fucking up — one way or another — because that was the only way Osho could get us to look at ourselves.

Anyway, after Sheela herself had left the Ranch, Osho sent a personal message to me that I was invited back, but somehow the news never reached me. I didn't find out about it for a long time — those were pre-internet days and emails hadn't been invented.

Later, when I was told, I remember saying to myself, "I'm actually kind of glad I didn't get that message, because I would have gone back." And even though Sheela was no longer there, I don't know if I was capable of working in such a total, dedicated fashion.

Looking at that period in my life, I can honestly say that I learned a big lesson, because now I know how to love the work I do — like writing this book, for example. Everything in its right time, right?

So, I don't want to present myself as a fantastic, devoted disciple and Sheela as a piece of shit. Basically, we were both shit, you know? I was shit because I wasn't ready to throw myself into work and she was shit because she wasn't ready to throw herself into meditation. It's kinda interesting.

Do I hate Sheela? Yes and no. If I met her in a bar, I'd sit down and have a drink with her, just as long as she wasn't the one mixing the cocktails. And, for sure, it would be an interesting "exchange of views" as they say when diplomats sit down to discuss disarmament with their enemies.

But, taking a wider view, Osho gave the Ranch to women to run. What became clear to me is that women were not capable of managing power any better than men. Sheela failed on the Ranch as I would have failed.

Without meditation, power corrupts, which makes me scratch my head and wonder: with meditation, would power corrupt or not? I don't know, because that scenario hasn't yet been documented. Maybe this is Day One of a new experiment. Somebody, please begin.

One footnote I forgot to mention: When I packed my bags and was ready to catch a bus to Venice, California, where my friend and lawyer Deva offered to put me up, I was given a ride out of Rajneeshpuram by the same young gentleman who had given me the news that my ass was grass and Sheela was my lawnmower. I asked him shyly if there was a reason. Instead of being honest, he suggested it was because I kissed a gal on the lips. (At this time, Osho had insisted we not kiss and also wear plastic gloves and condoms when we made love, to prevent the spread of AIDS. My god. I decided to forget making love as I was clumsy enough with my bare hands…let alone covered in plastic!) But I had to laugh out loud. Recently, during a drive-by (when Osho would drive one of his 93 Rolls-Royces for us to dance and sing and greet him along our road), a young lady got me confused with my friend Deben and gave me a big kiss. This Deben was my doppelganger...no kidding. She was so embarrassed, but the damage had been done.

When I later found out that my phone had been tapped and I realized this girl was not the real reason I was asked to leave the Ranch, I tried to get in touch with her — but by then she had married my doppelganger.

You win some and you lose some. Oh well.

Chapter Five

LOVE PLUS MEDITATION

Love is another name for life, another name for existence, another name for god. Don't condemn it, even if it exists on the lowest rung, because through condemnation you will not be able to transform it. Accept it as it is. Try to understand it. In that very understanding love starts changing: it starts going higher than lust. The more understanding grows, the higher love starts soaring. Love moves higher on the wings of understanding, on the wings of awareness, meditation.

Love plus meditation is equal to sannyas. Just make your love more and more meditative, wherever it is, and meditation will take it upwards. Meditation alone is without energy; love alone is without consciousness. They both need a co-operation, a deep co-operation. Osho

Meditation really means to love yourself. Love means to share yourself with someone else. Both are only techniques to bring you inside yourself. So, if you take your heartfelt feelings into meditation, you may never find that you are a meditator because you were built to be a lover. Or, if you are a lover and you go deep enough into your heartfelt feelings, you might find out you are a meditator.

In other words, it is always a risk to bring your heart into your meditation, it is a risk to move from meditation into your heart, but either way the outcome will be positive, because you have looked at yourself totally. You didn't look for a man to complete you, you didn't look for a woman to complete you. You looked at yourself to complete yourself, either through meditation or through love.

Both techniques can take you all the way into celebration. You cannot celebrate by drowning in your feelings and crying all the time. Neither can you celebrate by being an insensitive motherfucker cut off from feelings.

We need to look for that balance, both inside and outside, whether the balance is in you alone, or with your beloved. Otherwise, the game really is not worth playing. If you don't look deeply at your life, it is unlikely that your relationships will prove to be very fulfilling. Of course, if you do look deeply at your life, your relationships may still not work, but you will be more clear why you got involved in the first place.

As a wise man once told me: make as many mistakes as you want but always keep them brand new. Always bring your awareness into every situation. Every time you fall in love, keep watching what happens.

Remember, if you want to get married because you are in love, that is very different from getting married to find out if love works. Love does not work after you get married. Love works before you get married and then continues while you are married.

Anyway, as you probably guessed, this book is not about forever marriages. This book is about forever love, and that may take different forms with different people. You may like chocolate ice cream one day and vanilla ice cream another day, or you may end up saying this ice cream flavor isn't going to last for the rest of my life.

Have you ever thought about it? The concept that marriage means forever does not come from you and your personal experience. The concept comes from your parents. You didn't come up with it yourself. Love always happens here and now, in the present. It doesn't say anything about the future, yet somehow we're supposed to stay together until death do us part.

The cosmic joke is that some marriages actually do last forever and sometimes love also lasts forever. But this is life making fun of us because life, or existence, would never say that marriage does not last, it wants you to find out yourself.

So, existence has a good time laughing at us by creating a couple of people per million of the population, who really can make marriage last a lifetime. Even if they are codependent and driving each other crazy, it works.

Marriage is almost an impossible thing. When you think in terms of forever or, more accurately speaking, for the rest of one lifetime, there are maybe one or two couples in a whole city who can do it. But in your mind, everybody is like that, because that's the gold standard, that's the dream society holds out to you, like a carrot in front of an ass.

This book is about aloneness. There are couples who are alone together and that might seem a contradiction in terms and prevent this book from being the truth. However, the goal of this book is not to reveal the truth, the goal of the book is to help you discover who are you.

Are you here to be with somebody else to complete you, or are you enough unto yourself, in which case if you do meet a beloved she will complement who you are. She won't complete you, because that's already happened. Instead, she holds your hand and celebrates with you and makes you even more receptive to love – I have seen couples who like each other that much.

Whatever happens, aloneness is the only lasting reality that you will ever get to experience, so we will have to watch in this book to see if the path of aloneness leads you to be alone by yourself, or to be alone with somebody else.

But to be clear: when you meet someone like that, you will do it out of choiceless awareness, because it will be a gift from existence, out of abundance, not out of a desperate loneliness from your side. There is a difference between abundance and need.

And that is one of the qualities of meditation: you will come from your abundance of love, instead of the need to be with somebody. That is the whole essence of aloneness, to be yourself and then choose to be with someone or to be alone.

The two legs of meditation are to be alone and meditate, or to be so in love in your togetherness that you dissolve into oneness. All I am asking everybody who reads this book to ask themselves, as I've said before, is *Who am I?*

It is not to create dreams or expectations that end in disillusionment and pain. If the relationship dissolves, then it takes the form of two friends agreeing that we have been walking down the wrong path. Or maybe we really enjoyed walking down the path together, but now the path is dividing. Even though our love affair is over, we will continue to look at life together, connect sometimes, and support each other. It does not mean we have to always be in love.

Something that I have heard about my generation is that we invented "Living Apart Together." I like this concept. When some people hear about this concept, they think, *It seems we are no longer monogamous, so I can no longer trust him, I can no longer trust her.* But it is not like that at all; it is being so much in love that we can offer each other space, because I personally feel that my aloneness includes you.

But it also includes the fact that I might need my own room, or my own apartment. I think the two people who go into this process called Living Apart Together can have agreements: one can be monogamy; one can be financial; one can be meeting every Tuesday, Thursday, and Sunday.

Oftentimes, people live together not out of love, but out of financial convenience. And if you look at it and see that it is about finances, being aware that we are together because of those finances can sometimes create abundance. The funny thing is, abundance may bring you closer together and the thought of not living together may disappear.

Sometimes you need financial issues to see that you like living together. Sometimes you need finances to realize you want to be apart. I love this concept of Living Apart Together because it allows me both, to be alone and to have a beloved.

When I look at what makes me the happiest in this lifetime, it is when I am alone but I know that on Tuesday I am going to see my beloved, on Thursday we are going to movies. Oftentimes, I feel better when I am alone, knowing that I am in love, rather than when I am alone and on the hunt.

That hunt has turned out to be very exhausting for me. I think relaxing in love is a very beautiful experience. I think space is fantastic in a relationship. And sometimes space means the same room and sometimes it means two different apartments in two different cities. I don't know what you want; that is up to you.

A lot of times, I use myself as an example, hoping that you will tell me your own story. I hope as you read my book, you are writing your own life story. I always say that this book will be a success when you, the reader, can also write a book about your own experience of aloneness.

So what we are offering in this book is meditation, or let's call it the "Sword of Awareness." Oftentimes, people go to a therapist for years and years and nothing ever seems to get resolved, as if the therapist is just there to listen to you. In meditation, we talk about the Sword of Awareness: it cuts quickly and deeply. I offer this sword to you as a present to look at your own life.

"Be your own therapist" may be a new name for what is called meditation. I am my own therapist, but the outcome would be that the therapist in me died because the patient is healthy and does not need a doctor.

The Sword of Awareness is a technique for you to be your own therapist. Now, when you learn to be alone and enjoy it, the therapist just disappears, he does not even die, he just disappears.

In a sense, you are killing the dream in you. And once you kill the dream that you need help from anybody else, you wake up and the therapist is no longer there. So it would be a good technique to just ask yourself, *Do I need a therapist today? Can I count on myself?*

For example, when you get angry, you find you are watching yourself being angry and, in the watching, the anger slowly begins to disappear. And that is beautiful, especially if the person with whom you are angry can see your anger falling to the ground.

Seeing this, he says to himself, *Wow, she just dropped the anger. I have to do that too.* A special time when you have the opportunity to notice that you are no longer angry is at the end of Dynamic Meditation. You became angry in the second stage, when you had permission to let out your emotional pressure. Then, by stage five, not even half an hour later, you are dancing and celebrating.

I have spoken to doctors and therapists about this and suggested to them that, rather than being far apart, anger and joy live next door to each other in your brain and in your mind. The more anger you can express and the more tension you can let go, the more joy will follow. Before going further, I need to tell you a little more about Dynamic Meditation. I know,

I described it in my previous book, but it is such an incredible technique that I feel like telling it again.

Dynamic is done early, preferably when the night is ending and the morning is just beginning. So, you start this meditation in the dark and end in the light — it's kinda symbolic. In the ashram in India, this means getting out of bed at 5:30 am, carefully stepping over your sleeping girlfriend, brushing your teeth, walking to the ashram, and being in the meditation hall by 6:00.

Entering the hall, you pause to grab a tissue and blow your nose, because you're about to do a lot of intense breathing and you don't want any gloopy stuff in your nose to come flying out.

Dynamic begins with a loud gong, followed by rapid drumming music, and everyone starts breathing like crazy: Deep, fast, chaotic breathing through the nose, emphasizing the exhale.

For ten minutes, you do this and because it's done through the nose, this somehow prevents hyperventilation, which might easily happen if you did the same thing through your mouth. You don't start feeling dizzy, faint, woozy or weak. You may want to stop, but that's just because you're lazy and have a mental image of how nice it would be to still be in bed with your girlfriend.

If you do this breathing technique with totality, you build up emotional pressure inside, maybe feeling angry or irritated by this strange activity. Also, because there's usually a guy up front, on the , urging you on and shouting "Go for it! Be total! Keep going!" which usually makes me want to punch him out.

Feeling mad is a good start, really, because after ten minutes there's another loud gong and everyone goes crazy. I mean really! You've never seen anything like it. Of course, you're not supposed to peek — in fact, lots of people are wearing blindfolds. But if you do look around, the whole room has become a madhouse.

People are screaming, yelling, beating the air with their fists, pounding pillows, crying and sobbing into their hands, wailing, complaining, cursing, curling up on the floor in the fetal position like they've just been born.

Expression is the name of the game. Let it out! It's rare in life that we get the time, space and invitation to throw aside our social politeness, good manners, and carefully groomed behavior. Remember all those times you had to bite back your words, or be polite when you were seething inside, or when you had to smile and sit on your shit?

Not this time. Boom! Take the lid off Pandora's box and let out the monsters that have been chained up inside you. Just don't use proper words. Use sounds, but if something sounding like "motherfucker" slips out, don't worry, everyone is making so much noise they'll never hear it or figure out who said it.

Ten minutes flies by, another gong, and it's time for a new stage. Immediately, everyone stops screaming and starts jumping up and down with arms raised, shouting the mantra "Hoo! Hoo! Hoo!" No, really, I'm serious. You can't make this stuff up. It's for real.

Let me tell you, there are people on this planet who can energetically and enthusiastically jump off the ground for ten minutes with their arms in the air shouting "Hoo!" and never take a break. Alas, I am not one of them. At least, not now. Maybe I was, 48 years ago.

Fortunately, there are other ways. For example, when it gets too much, you can keep your feet on the ground and pump your hips, thrusting them forwards each time you yell "Hoo!" Or you can rise up on your toes, then bang your heels down rhythmically on the ground, each time yelling "Hoo!" The main thing is to keep going and preferably to keep on jumping as long as is humanly possible.

The general idea in the third stage is to hammer the energy stored in your sex center in two ways: when your heels hit the ground it sends a shock wave up your legs to your genital area, while the sound "Hoo!" is supposed to do the same from the other direction. In this meditation, the sex center is seen as a reservoir of locked-in energy that can be released and spread all over your body.

By the way, there is loud music supporting each of the three stages and it really helps to get you through. The group energy also helps. And yes, the guy on the mike urging you on, he also helps.

Then finally, after 30 minutes of this super-intense activity, just when you're convinced you're about to experience a major cardiac arrest, the music suddenly stops and a single magical word is broadcast loud and clear "STOP!"

And you stop. Just stop. That's all you do... stop. No itching, no scratching, no rubbing your nose, no wiping sweat off your eyes and definitely no sitting nor lying down.

Osho says, "This is the moment when meditation can happen."

Why now? Because you have just spent 30 minutes emptying your mind and exhausting your body. How does that help? Well, as Osho sees it, and I have to say it's also my own experience, the state of meditation cannot be "done." You can't get there by doing.

The American Dream tells you that whatever you want in life, you can get it. Just do it. And that is exactly what you cannot do when exploring the most essential phenomenon on this planet: meditation.

Meditation descends on you, or opens up within you, when you are empty, silent and receptive. That's why we "do" so much beforehand. If you "do" the first three stages properly, you are so utterly finished that you just cannot do any more. In this exhausted and empty state, meditation has a chance to possess you and embrace you with all its stillness, silence and infinite inner space.

Okay, time passes and after 15 minutes soft music begins to play. In this, the final and fifth stage, you are invited to dance freely, any style you like, any way you feel.

At the end, the music fades and you walk out into the sunshine, slightly dazed and confused, but feeling pleasantly awakened, refreshed and energized. For a while, at least, your mind is quiet. If you happen to be in India, may I suggest that a cup of chai will complete the meditation experience.

So, this is why I said to you that anger and joy live next door to each other inside you. You don't think about it at the time, because you're so involved in the meditation. But looking back on your morning's Dynamic experience, you notice that, yes, in stage two I was really angry, wanting to kill someone, and then, a few minutes later in stage five, I was dancing and feeling joyful.

In this joyful mood, instead of directing anger towards anyone else, you thank that person. You thank your boyfriend or girlfriend for having given you the opportunity to be angry. You thank the rickshaw driver who ripped you off for 20 rupees when the fare to the resort was only ten.

And when I say "thank you," I mean that you own your anger. Once you own your own anger, it is easy to feel the Sword of Awareness operating in your life, and then you can be your own therapist, you can let go of old resentments and give yourself more time and space to be joyous.

Most probably, you have never heard of the Ho'oponopono Ritual. But I have and what's more I'm also pretty sure I know how to spell it, which for a guy who never listened in high school is pretty impressive.

When I first heard about Ho'oponopono I was told it originated in Hawaii but then I discovered that similar rituals are found all over the Pacific, so basically it's an ancient Polynesian cultural technique for healing families and dealing with social problems.

The essence of this ritual is to say: "I am sorry. Please forgive me. Thank you. I love you." It's a way of saying "thank you" and owning your own emotions.

For example, your boyfriend is not you, but he is a great mirror, and in that mirror you may see anger. Maybe, if you look a little deeper in the mirror, you will realize, *My gosh, I don't need the mirror, I am just angry*.

If you never see that the mirror is not you, if you never see that your boyfriend or girlfriend is not you, the chances are you're going to end the relationship and only then you may find out, *My god, it was not him, it was me*. But then it's too late and you can't get him or her back in your life.

So my feeling is that when someone pushes your buttons, annoys you, irritates you, you should always look for that place in yourself where you can say, "Thank you for making me aware that my anger is not your problem. Please forgive me, I am sorry and I love you." And that is why Ho'oponopono is such a beautiful technique.

I'll give you the structure for Ho'oponopono and take you through it, but first let me back up and explain the context: Ho'oponopono translates simply as "correction." In many Polynesian cultures, it is believed that a person's errors, such as anger or misconduct, cause illness. For example, if a child falls ill, the parents are suspected of quarrelling.

The therapy that cures this sickness is confession. The patient, or a family member, needs to admit his responsibility. If no one confesses, the sickness may continue. Some Polynesian people believe that secrecy is what gives power to illness. When the error is confessed, it no longer has power over the person.

More recently, the ritual has been adapted into a wider problem-solving process and as a form of self-help therapy. The idea has been developed that meditators can reach a "zero state" of no limits, no memories, and no identity through reciting the mantra "I love you. I'm sorry. Please forgive me. Thank you."

Here is the ritual. You're welcome to try it. If you need a time structure, I would suggest five or ten minutes per stage, but feel free to create a timing that suits you.

Step 1: Repentance – *SAY: I'M SORRY*

The first step is to realize that you are responsible for everything in your mind. Once you accept this, it's natural to feel sorry. A good exercise is to choose something that you already know is your own responsibility, that you have created in yourself. Overweight? Addicted to nicotine, or alcohol? Do you have anger or self-esteem issues? Start there and say you are sorry. Just say "I'M SORRY." That's it! It is even more powerful to say, "I realize that I am responsible for this issue in my life and I feel remorse that my consciousness has allowed it."

Step 2: Ask Forgiveness – SAY: PLEASE FORGIVE ME

Don't worry about to whom you are asking. Just ask: "PLEASE FORGIVE ME." Say it over and over. Mean it. Remember your remorse from Step One as you ask to be forgiven.

Step 3: Gratitude – SAY: THANK YOU

Say "THANK YOU" – again, it doesn't really matter who or what you are thanking. Thank your body for all it does for you. Thank yourself for being the best you can be. Thank God. Thank the Universe. Thank whatever it was that just forgave you. Just keep saying "THANK YOU."

Step 4: Love – SAY: I LOVE YOU

Say "I LOVE YOU." Say it to your body, say it to God, say it to the universe. Say "I LOVE YOU" to the air you breathe, to the house that shelters you. Say "I LOVE YOU" to your challenges and to your mistakes and successes. Say it over and over. Just say "I LOVE YOU" and mean it. There is nothing as powerful as love.

Ho'oponopono is simple. When you look in the mirror offered by this ritual, you see yourself. This can be painful, so learn to love and accept yourself. Remember, it's all very well saying "I love you" to your friends, family and neighbors, but the very first step which makes all of this possible is to learn to love yourself.

Chapter Six

DROWN YOURSELF

Start meditating. Start putting off the constant chattering of the head. Slowly, the mind becomes quiet. Get into things where the mind is not needed—for example, dancing. Dance, and dance to abandon, because in dance the mind is not needed. You can lose yourself in a dance. In losing yourself in a dance, the heart will start functioning again. Drown yourself in music. And slowly you will see that there is a totally different world of the heart. And in the heart there is always trust. The heart does not know how to doubt, just as the mind does not know how to trust. Osho

There's an acronym in modern American culture called KISS. I love it. As you probably know, it means "Keep It Simple Stupid." When something is complicated, maybe that is not the time to make a decision. Instead, see if you can melt it down into something new and simple. The way I see it, KISS is another term for witnessing and watching your own life.

The first time I heard KISS, apart from the other meaning, which I learned much earlier in whispers from my giggling sisters, the clarification came from my father. He was trying to help me get a grip on life and I discovered that KISS was a pretty good idea.

So, as I made my way towards adulthood, I tried to keep it simple and later added what Gurdjieff said, "When somebody insults you and makes you angry, give yourself 24 hours before reacting."

Of course, it doesn't always work. Sometimes we enjoy being too emotional, too excited, to wait 24 hours and we don't want to keep it simple. We want to keep it exciting and do something or make a decision right now. We are going to have a good time tonight but tomorrow we will probably wake up and say, *What the fuck happened to me?*

The issue is impatience. The impulse is impulsiveness. The thing is, you have the same problem as an Arab boy in the desert of Morocco, who one day felt so desperate about his life that he jumped off his camel, kneeled in the sand, raised his eyes and arms towards heaven and cried:

"God, my life is fucked, I am in love with a beautiful girl but her parents say I can't marry her until I have money. Now, my boss has fired me and I just want to die. I am so in love, but I can't do anything about it."

The boy is so passionate about his pain that God actually shows up and says to the boy:

"Be patient, talk to your boss, try and do better at work, and stop thinking about that girl while you're supposed to be working. Do so well that you get a raise, then you can afford to be married and then enjoy life and don't bring your work home to your bedroom. In other words, be total in everything you do."

The boy was delighted and he thanked God. By the way, yesterday God was in one religion and today he is in another religion. He tends to wear a different hat every day and enjoys himself, hoping that one day you realize you are God, God is you, you are you, and the only religion worthy of the name is KISS.

Anyway, the boy was very pleased. God gave him the right answer based on patience, time, and love. He got his job back, saved money, won over the girl's parents, and married her.

So God was very surprised to see this boy, one day, standing alone in the desert, shaking his fist at the sky. And God said,

"Hey, I just helped you out of a tight spot! How come you are mad at me?" The boy answered, "I started to pray and my camel just ran off!"

God replied to him,

"Listen, I am God, not a camel caretaker. I can help you, but that doesn't mean you are helpless and cannot take care of yourself. Next time you pray, tether your camel first."

Life is pretty simple. A lot of it is about looking in the mirror and keeping the mirror as clean as possible. Usually, when you look in the mirror, it is held by somebody else and you find yourself looking at who you think you are, based on that person's reflection of you.

You look at your wife to find out who you are. You look at your mother to find out who you are. You look at your boss to find out who you are. And the truth of the matter is, you have to let go of these reflections in all of these mirrors. You have to let go of your self-image, as created by your wife, your mother and your children, and trust that being more authentic can bring them back to you in a new way.

Eventually, when you look in the mirror, you will see yourself alone, as you really are. This can be painful, because most people when they look in the mirror, don't like what they see. They see someone who is getting older, who is overweight, who has greying hair and wrinkles.

It takes time to be reborn. By the time you feel yourself as a human being with a soul, you might be middle-aged and a bit overweight.

My suggestion is that when you look in the mirror, resist the temptation to freeze. The mirror always reflects back what it sees and so, if you look in the mirror frozen, if you look in the mirror without loving yourself, this will be reflected back. And yes, it can be painful.

So, one of the suggestions I have is: always move when you look in the mirror, always dance when you look in the mirror. Unless, of course, you are trying to pull a hair off the end of your nose with a pair of tweezers, in which case I suggest you stand perfectly still until the operation has been successfully accomplished.

You catch my drift? I don't want you to fake it, but I'm suggesting you might experiment a little and dance in front of your mirror. Show the mirror how much you love yourself.

Now, I want you to start doing what many people in the East do: they only eat three quarters of any meal, they never go back for second helpings, and they always leave the table a little bit hungry.

What happens when you leave the table with your stomach filled to capacity, feeling like you're big enough to burst? It's going to make you feel hungry as soon as it's just a little bit empty and you will feel the urge to eat again, even though there is no need. A lean belly, on the other hand, won't make you feel hungry if it's properly fed. It's all psychological, nothing to do with nutrition.

We need to add some discipline to our lives, and the good news is that once you start to meet yourself you don't need as much food. Maybe adding discipline means leaving the table a little bit hungry so you can watch your stomach shrink. So, keep looking at yourself, moving more, eating less.

Remember to forgive yourself for having an emotional body that has a tremendous need to feel fulfilled, not necessarily by food but also by love. In fact, as we all know, when we're in love we can easily forget to eat, lose our appetite. Why? Because the emotional body is already fulfilled.

It's my intuitive feeling that the same principle can be applied to self-love. As you fall in love with yourself, you may not be as hungry as before. It would be nice, right? Try and see if it works. I can't guarantee. I am a little bit overweight myself because, after all, I also have an emotional body.

What does this mean, "emotional body"? Well, I have esoteric friends who tell me that it exists as a field of subtle energy, suffusing through the physical body and extending a few centimeters beyond it. They also say it has its own energy center, or chakra, located in the lower belly.

All I know is that my emotions have a life of their own, they have needs of their own. Sometimes they are hard to control, sometimes they overwhelm me, and love and food are two overlapping ways of responding to the same emotional needs. That's why people who are longing for love tend to eat chocolate as a substitute. It fills a hole in the emotional body. The good news is that loving yourself also fills the same hole.

These days, everybody is looking for new alternatives to lose weight. Well, maybe I'm onto something here. I could start a franchise and run TV commercials:

"Fall in love with yourself today and lose ten pounds in six weeks!"

Once you begin to feel okay with yourself, you have a chance to lose more than just physical weight. You lose religious weight, because you are freeing yourself from any kind of belief system and dropping all those sermons, all those commandments, all those "shoulds" and "should nots."

You also lose political weight, because even though you want to be sure to vote for the good guy you know he's not going to be your savior. You don't carry the burden of hope. You're not waiting for the Age of Aquarius to dawn in the United States before celebrating your life.

When you look in the mirror, I don't want you to look at your self-criticism and your desire to be thinner, I want you to look at the question "What would I look like if I was already enlightened?"

Then you come up with your inner weight. You have an inner weight, which is who you are as an enlightened being, participating in this lifetime as a free person, and you have an outer weight which is the weight you have right now from never asking yourself, "Who am I?"

The cosmic joke of this book is, even when you become enlightened, you will still have a body, but that body will start to sing, dance, feel, and love like a new person.

This book is about breathing in, into your human doer, and breathing out, into your human being. Then you begin to look like yourself, you begin to act like yourself, you begin to dance like yourself. It is very exciting.

By the way, you don't necessarily need to share any of this until you have thoroughly embodied it, in other words, until it is you. There's no need to tell your friends, "Guess what Krishna Prem said!" Chances are, your friends will see it anyway, in the light in your eyes and the inner smile behind your face.

Only then you can share, preferably without words, because words tend to destroy the truth. From the mouths of the awakened, words can point towards the truth, but, for the most part, when a person is speaking he is destroying the truth.

Find out what your true body weight is. Stand in front of the mirror, send loving energy to your physical body and tell it kindly, "You can let go. Now you don't have to protect me so much." And you will lose weight.

It works both ways: if you feel better, you will lose a kilo. If you lose a kilo, you will feel better. You can do it through discipline or through loving yourself. It is just the natural thing.

So basically, as the Zen mystics say, you have an original face and that face is who you are before you had a body. It is also who you are during the time you have a body, and it is also who you are when you leave your body. The body that you are so identified with, the religion that you are so identified with, the parents who you are so identified with, they have nothing to do with you. Well, okay, they do, but only for a while.

What I'm saying is: one day, you will not have a body, you will not have parents, and you will not have a religion. And that is okay, because it is how you came here. So we need to trust a little bit that we are one with the universe, which means that we are not necessarily one with the United States, Germany, Russia, Uzbekistan, or wherever your physical body happened to be born in this particular incarnation.

Somehow, we have created all these nations as extensions of our need for a personal identity. But these are just lines on a map and, in spite of what it says in your passport, they actually don't exist.

As Yuri Gagarin, the first man in space, said when he looked out of his satellite window at the view below him, "My beloved Earth." He didn't say "My beloved Russia." He saw the whole undivided unity of the planet.

These nations have a purpose politically and economically, but they may not serve your best interests as a seeker of truth. When you realize this, you may want to change those lines on the map, but you may also find this to be too big a project for one awakened individual.

On the other hand, you may find it very easy to change yourself, and once you change yourself, then you can easily have compassion for other people because they believe in those lines on the map and mostly have little or no idea what inner life is all about.

In your short lifetime, I hesitate to recommend that you try to enlighten everybody about this radical concept of ours, that all distinctions are creating unnecessary separation. The effort required will occupy a great deal of your time, you will be mistaken for some kind of missionary or nutcase, and the upshot, in all likelihood, will be a door slammed in your face.

You and I know that distinctions prevent unity and they do no good at all, unless you have a sense of humor, which, by the way, is a really important spiritual quality and extremely valuable. The more awakened you become, the greater your need to see the cosmic joke.

If you have a sense of humor, if you are almost enlightened, if you meditate and explore inside yourself, then you will see that being American, Mexican, or Brazilian is just a form of clothing; being Catholic, Protestant, or Greek Orthodox is just a form of clothing; even being a woman or man is just clothing.

The thing about wearing these kinds of clothes is that you need to know how to take them off and how to put them on. I am talking about witnessing; I am talking about having fun as a half-awake human being on a planet filled with sleepy people. It sounds elitist, sure, but what can I do? I have to say it the way it is.

When I say you are not the body, I don't mean you can't put it back on for fun. I simply mean that the identification you once had with your body is broken. Now, you might think, once you know you are not the body, there's no reason to care about it so much, so you may as well sit in front of the TV and eat ice cream all day long.

No, no, no, I didn't say that! Your body is your temple. Your body is the vehicle through which you get to experience life in all its myriad forms. Your body needs care and respect and love.

Strangely, this is hard for some people to understand, because they think that once they meditate, once they see the body as a "leather bag filled with filth," as some religious ascetics have called it, then you can ignore it and abuse it. After all, why bother to look after this poor costume of rags and bones, when it's going to grow old, sick, wither and die?

This negative attitude is very ancient. You can find it in all the religions: monks and sadhus and yogis who condemn the body and its simple pleasures, because of its fleeting nature. I take the opposite view: treat your body even better now, because you know it is the temple of your consciousness.

If you don't love your body, you'll find it's not as easy to meditate as it is when you love your body. You don't need to identify with it, but you also don't need to abuse it.

Your body is always going to ask, "Give me a baby, give me a meal, give me a religion."

You have to say to your body, "I am so happy to be in this temple, and I promise you I will take good care of it, but when I am alone in my room, when I am meditating, I am not going to allow you to tell me that the body is more important than it is.

"As soon as I leave the room, you can say to me, 'Hey, I want to look good. And I want to have fun.' Then I will laugh with you and we will go out and enjoy ourselves. So, give me an hour a day to be without you being important, and for the other 23 hours I will take care of you effortlessly."

Let's take the risk of being innocent. Let's take the risk of not making our minds and our bodies so important. Remind your children not to get too hung up on physical appearances – even though, when you're a teenager and desperate to impress your peers, you think it's the end of the world if you happen to get a single zit.

At first, there is identification, with little or no distance. The appearance of your body seems to be everything, the ideas in your mind and the feelings in your heart likewise. What can be more important in the universe than your first love affair? Even if God himself came to pay you a visit, you'd have to tell him, "I'm on the phone to Sandy right now, can you come back in an hour please?"

As you get a little older, you start to get a different perspective. Actually, that is when you become interested in meditation and the witness can be born. When you say, "Aha, being a young man, a young woman, has been great, but now I seem to be moving into a different phase."

By the way, like I said in the very beginning, when you are in the business of cleaning your basement, you need to find that innocence in yourself, when you were a child, and bring it with you into your adult life. Normally, we think it's okay to forget about childhood qualities such as innocence because you can't make money with them. They don't do particularly well on Wall Street when the bulls are charging or the bears are feeding.

But when you learn to meditate, when you discover the witness inside, you also realize that it requires a childlike quality, an innocence, a freshness, which is also known in Zen as "beginner's mind."

In my opinion, this is the definition of meditation; to be a child with awareness. To have that same innocence and enthusiastic attitude to life as you did when you were very young, without being foolish about it, just celebrating how amazing it is to be alive and bringing your awareness to it.

But not the awareness you learned at school. That's not awareness. That's knowledge, that's information. I am talking about regaining the awareness of a child who was so happy to be alive, and then celebrating this quality throughout your entire life.

Chapter Seven

RADIATE LOVE

Sitting alone in your room, be loving. Radiate love. Fill the whole room with your love energy. Feel vibrating with a new frequency, feel swaying as if you are in the ocean of love. Create vibrations of love energy around you. And you will start feeling immediately that something is happening, something in your aura is changing, something around your body is changing; a warmth is arising around your body...a warmth like deep orgasm. You are becoming more alive. Something like sleep is disappearing. Something like awareness is arising. Osho

The buddhas are asking us to love, to love ourselves and watch. Don't just love. Don't just watch. If you watch without loving, you will most probably fall asleep. If you love without watching, you will end up abusing love.

So, for us, in this book, the balance is found in loving ourselves and watching. We need to remember the mixed metaphor of having "roots and wings," which means being firmly rooted in the ground like trees while at the same time having wings to fly into the open sky like eagles. We need to be firmly planted in the ground and reaching up to love.

There's a beautiful anecdote about Van Gogh in which some people looking at his paintings objected that the trees he painted seemed to grow so high they went beyond the stars. To which Van Gogh replied, "It is the longing of every tree to touch the stars." Actually Van Gogh was talking about himself. It's not just true about trees. It is the longing of every human spirit to fulfill its destiny.

There is an energy field all around us, from six feet below your feet to six feet above your head, a whole energy field of love. What love needs though, is participation. In order to be thrilled with this life, you need to participate, you need to swim in the ocean of existence, just like a fish in the ocean.

The fish in the ocean does not even know where the ocean is, he is so accustomed to being in the ocean. The only exceptions I can think of are to be found in the Pixar-Disney cartoon film, *Finding Nemo*, where part of the story focuses on the Tank Gang who, confined in a fish tank in a dentist's office in Sydney, Australia, are desperate to escape and return to the ocean.

Loved that movie, by the way. The only thing that gave me anxiety was the way those courageous little guys in the Tank Gang who'd made it all the way from the dentist's office to the ocean were left floating on the surface inside their plastic bags. Come on, Walt. If you allow them get that far you should have the decency to pop their bags and let them swim in the ocean. But I digress. The energy field surrounding us is almost like an outer witness, an extension of our consciousness, so let's say you are surrounded by an energy body. For the esoteric people reading this book, we might call it the "esoteric body" and it extends further than the emotional body we talked about earlier. By the way, there are seven of these subtle bodies altogether, but we don't need to know them all.

Usually, you are in the mind when you read a book, so remember I am not asking you to think about all these concepts and work anything out. I am asking you to be in a state of No Mind. I want you to just breathe in and breathe out, accepting that you have an energy field that we might call "the witness."

There's no need to look for this energy body, just use it. Just get out and play, go out and dance and feel your energy expanding. When it has expanded enough, then you can sit down, relax and meditate. But don't meditate before you feel thoroughly revitalized and alive.

It is great to be under 30 years old and explore your energy in this expansive way, but it is exhausting for a guy like me, now that I am well over 70. I am exhausted by doing, doing, doing. I am a guy that is about being, being, being.

However, it's all very well talking about swimming in the ocean, but let's also be practical and remember the first thing you need to do – like I said before – is go down and clean your basement. This is what we call our primal deconditioning; we need to go into the basement, into our unconscious and shine a light there. This is what enlightenment means.

It means taking a light into your own unconscious mind and watching darkness disappear because, as we all know, darkness always disappears in the presence of light. The problem is that nobody wants to bring light into the basement, because that is where we find all the shit – excuse my French, *s'il vous plaît*. Like I said before, this is where all your hurt is, where all your wounds are.

But when we bring the light in, everything miraculously begins to heal, just by shining some light on your pain. It is you that is in pain, nobody is doing it to you. Maybe years ago there were people like your parents, for example, who unintentionally caused you pain when you were a little child, but now it's just you.

This understanding helps you to take responsibility for your wounds and begin the healing process. I think of it as bringing in the light. I bring light into meeting my little Michael, which was my name given by my parents before I became Krishna, and I meet him there, in the basement, knowing that my little boy has his own history and his own wounds.

I hold his hand and say, "I feel more courageous now that I am aware of the pain that you went through — we can walk through the basement, we can clean up our act, we can heal, I am not going to let anybody hurt you anymore, and we are going to discuss why we got hurt and how much fear we have. And we are going to giggle and we are going to live, we are going to dance and we are going to get better…we are going to get better."

This is the process of healing your inner child and then, once you have completed with that work, you can walk up to the attic of your house, where meditation leads you out into the open sky just above the roof.

But if you go into your attic without having a good foundation, without having cleaned your basement, you will find it difficult to fly out the skylight. So, first we need to walk down into the basement, take that little boy's hand, and then beat the crap out of all the people who have been sitting on us, all the while thanking them for their good intentions, even though those good intentions crippled us and caused us pain.

The basement is a great place when it's clean and, metaphorically speaking, you don't have to go beyond this primal deconditioning in order to have a good life. But if you want an easy entry into meditation, then, like I say, you need to walk up to the attic and let your Buddha Nature start to shine. The Buddha can't shine if he is distracted by pain. When you clean up your basement, you start to heal and your Buddha Nature begins to shine.

Once you have learned to meditate and when you feel comfortable in your own skin, then any time you like you can walk down from the attic, go into your living room, relax and have a beer.

You can say, "Wow, I know now that I am a buddha. Now I just feel like sitting on the sofa and having a beer in front of the fireplace."

And once in a while you can look at your children and say, "I'm not going to do that

stuff to you that was done to Michael, I am going to give you space."

You can also look at your wife and say, "Yes, we got married because I needed to be with somebody. But now that I am ready to be alone, I just want to thank you. And if we can both grow up, if we can do our homework, I think we can be very good friends."

A friendship can come without a hard beginning. When two people meet at 27 years old, they can barely get out of bed, but when they are 54 years old, they can barely get into bed. I think the friendship that comes out of love is fantastic. Osho always used to say that freedom is a higher value than love. Love is often a very hot, sexy space while freedom is a very cool space. Freedom means that I have moved from passion to compassion, from lust to trust, and it is a beautiful thing.

Friendship that comes out of sex can be good. I don't trust platonic relationships too much, because it always feels like something is missing and sometimes there is just not enough energy to work with. I do trust heat and responding to the body's natural impulses, and when you finally move beyond all the huffing and puffing a real friendship can emerge from it.

Osho spoke a lot about friendliness and one day he said to me, "I would love to be a friend to you, but you need to be worthy of friendship; friendship means you have done your homework. Now we can see each other's Buddha Nature and we know we are the same."

Osho added, "Friendship does not mean you can sit on the podium with me and do the talking in morning discourse. I don't want to be a guru but I can see that you still want to be one, so I do the talking. Even though we are friends, I am still going to do the talking."

When you move into compassion you can clearly see how people can push your buttons, which is a fun way of saying they can upset you, make you angry, trigger your emotions. Now you can thank your friends for pushing your buttons. As long as they can push your buttons, you are not ready, your basement and your attic are not clean.

When someone really insults you, of course, you get crazy and want to kill the person, but please refrain. When in jail, you fail. Instead, meditate over it for 24 hours. I can just about add a "thank you" to a button-pushing situation where I tell the person, "I had no idea how upset I am. I have learned through compassion that I need to work on this, and I want to thank you for bringing it up so I can work on it." Then, after thanking them, feel free to kick them in the butt – no, really, I'm kidding.

The next time your friend pushes your buttons, you may laugh and say "Thank you." And the final outcome of compassion is that you have no more buttons that can be pushed.

Now, you have to be ready for this new situation because as soon as your buttons can't be pushed, you will be tempted to think your journey on the KP Express is over and you've arrived at Self-Actualization Junction. First, it's probably not true. Second, the risk now is that you will yawn, scratch your head and find yourself getting very bored.

At this point you need to see that boredom is a misunderstanding. You need to realize how much energy there is here, in this new state of not getting your buttons pushed. Everybody knows how much energy you can feel when you are upset and pissed off. But how many people know how much energy there is, when you are in a great space?

Compassion is cool, not hot, but if you can become aware, it is also delightful. That would be one of the desirable outcomes of this book, that you are delighted to be cool. Cool is cool, if you catch my drift. These are things I could say in a hundred different ways, but it is only theoretical bullshit until you get it.

So this book is an indication that you, too, can be thrilled with this lifetime. But I can't do your homework for you. And even if you hate this book, who cares? I already pocketed the money you paid for it, so I don't really care that you might not get it in this moment. But if it is a good book, which I think it is, then maybe two years from now you will exclaim, "Hey, Krishna Prem was right! He's not a dickhead after all. I just got it! I wish I hadn't given that book away."

But I am glad you did give this book away. Because once you get it, you don't need this book. You only need books until you get it. Once you get it, a book is just a paperweight. You don't need it, you don't need me, you only need you.

You don't need my book, you need your own book. You can drop my book because it is not your book. But if you drop your book, when you let go of your old story, when you trust this moment, that is when your life begins.

Start to enjoy yourself. And like I say, the first thing you need to do is fall in love with yourself. Not with your wife, not with your parents, and not with your children. You need to learn to fall in love with yourself. And by the way, I am not suggesting you kill your parents, or get divorced, or tell your kids they are horrible.

What I mean is, you can fall in love with yourself now. The beauty of this is that, once you fall in love with yourself, you may fall in love with your wife for the first time, you may say to your parents, "Thank you," for the first time in a long time. It does not change your life, it changes you. Maybe afterwards you decide to change your life, but that's just a by-product.

I remember Osho saying that if you don't love yourself then, when somebody else loves you, you are going to think they are trying to fool you, because you think you are not good enough for them to love you.

Once I start asking myself who I am, my wife might run away, saying, "I was in love with a dream. I can't handle reality!" It is a risky business to get real, because your wife might not like your kind of real. But the truth of the matter is that everybody is real, pretending to be unreal. The essence of this book is that everybody is enlightened pretending to be asleep.

So, the cosmic joke is that when you wake up, you begin to celebrate and you begin to say "Thank you." However, until you wake up, I'm sorry to say most of us believe we are only alive because we feel the burden of the daily grind. When the heaviness of life seems to be dragging us down, when we feel that weight, we feel as if we know what life is.

This book is saying that you don't have any weight, that your life is about celebration, that once you take off your personality, you are weightless. Now, this can be very scary, because we have forgotten how to be comfortable in our own skin. We only know how to be comfortable when we have a plastic personality surrounding us, to the point where we think the plastic is inside of ourselves. We actually think we are plastic.

Remember that old fifties cartoon comic strip hero Plastic Man? Wow this dates me, but never mind. "Plas" was made totally of plastic and could reach around corners, stretch himself any which way, and rescue damsels in distress with his unbelievably long reach. He loved being plastic, but we don't. Not really. Therefore, it is my painful duty to ask you to peel off your plastic. It hurts, but it is worth it.

Even speaking is untruthful. In fact, this book is a lie until you are real. So, I don't want you to believe in this book, I want you to look at yourself and say, *Is this book talking to me?* Because we both know that Krishna Prem can't help you, this book can't help you.

The only thing that can help is if this book tickles you to ask the question "Who am I?" It may tickle you with pain, but it can also tickle you with delight. And the more you ask yourself, "Who am I?" the more your delight will outgrow your pain and give you the courage to go on, because you need courage.

Can you believe that? You need courage to be yourself! I mean, what kind of world do we live in, when it takes courage to say "I love myself"? How embarrassing is it to tell that to somebody? When you tell your girlfriend "I love myself" is she going to clap her hands with joy, or is she going to feel scared and start thinking, *What does he mean? Does that mean he does not love me anymore?*

On the contrary, when you say "I love myself" it gives everyone else room to have the same experience. And that is what you need to share with your intimate friends: "When I say this, I am including you."

I am tired of saying "I love you." If I drop the I, the YOU automatically drops and life becomes love. I don't love you because you are my girlfriend. I love you because we are holding hands and moving through this moment in spacetime together.

The way I like to see it: you are sitting on a mountain top thinking you are hot-shit stuff. You have a wife, you have a job, you have parents, you have a religion, and you are keeping it all together. But behind the act, secretly, deep down inside, you have the feeling that it is costing way too much effort, because you have to try so hard in order to keep your act together.

And I am telling you to let go, fall apart, just fall apart and trust that you are actually real. You don't need to put an act in order to be loved. We are all afraid of being vulnerable, wondering *Will she still love me if I am real? Will I still love myself if I am real?*

So, my feeling is very simple: you are on a mountain peak called personality and you need to go down into the valley. I mean, you need to tell your boss that you need to take time off, and you need to say to your religion, *If you are real, I will pick you up later on, once I am real.*

Everybody is going to be really scared when you do that, because they know they have been lying to you, just as much as you have been lying about your own life. In meditation, we call this process "entering the dark night of the soul" and we will go over it later in this book. Many people think that it's wrong to speak good about yourself and it's selfish to ask yourself, *Who am I?* But the truth is you need to love this feeling of falling in love with yourself before you can fall in love with anybody or anything.

Most people are trying to share with others before they have anything to share, that is how they end up sharing money instead of love. Everyone is afraid to love themselves. And by the way, it is painful to fall in love with yourself because everybody is going to encourage you to carry on with your great act, sitting on your mountaintop.

Your society is saying to you, "Forget about this selfishness and share, share, share!" The buddhas are saying the same thing with a different twist: "Carry on looking inside, find out who you are first, then share from who you are. No need to share from being wealthy and by starting charitable foundations, simply share yourself."

Unfortunately, we just don't have any training in unconditional love. For me, the family is conditional and that is wonderful, because you learn how to love your family. Let's say, for example, you have two parents, five siblings and a wife, so you love eight people. When you widen your vision to include this whole existence, there are seven billion people you don't love, because they are not your family.

Or maybe it's more than seven billion, I don't even know because everybody is having babies all the time, even now as we speak, and the line on the global graph keeps shooting upwards. Do you know it took two million years for the human population of this planet to reach one billion, and only two hundred years to reach seven billion? We're in trouble, but everybody's too busy counting likes on Facebook to notice.

You can't begin life without a family, but once you learn about meditation and witnessing, your consciousness will naturally want to expand to include an extended family of seven billion people. It's is not easy to think about how to love that many people, which is okay because you don't have to "do" it.

It is not about doing, it is about being. It is about being in love, or rather, about *being love*. So it is not about giving material things or about being personally intimate with everyone. You don't need to know them, you just live in a state of love that is all-inclusive. Just remember,

love needs to be celebrated and that's something everyone can do, enlightened or unenlightened, it makes no difference.

Before electricity was invented, monks in monasteries were faithfully copying the Bible in basements, working by dim candlelight, using ink and quill pens. So they kept writing "celibate, celibate, celibate..."

When electricity was created and the lights went on, they saw something else: "Oh, my God, we are missing the R!" They realized it should read: "celebrate, celebrate, celebrate"!

Chapter Eight
LOVE PLUS MEDITATION

Love is another name for life, another name for existence, another name for god. Don't condemn it, even if it exists on the lowest rung, because through condemnation you will not be able to transform it. Accept it as it is. Try to understand it. In that very understanding love starts changing: it starts going higher than lust. The more understanding grows, the higher love starts soaring. Love moves higher on the wings of understanding, on the wings of awareness, meditation.

Love plus meditation is equal to sannyas. Just make your love more and more meditative, wherever it is, and meditation will take it upwards. Meditation alone is without energy; love alone is without consciousness. They both need a co-operation, a deep co-operation. Osho

When I say "I love you," the most important thing for me is when the *I* drops away, and the *you* also drops away, and only love remains. Let's meditate over this for a moment. If you say "I love you," it is always nice to hear but it is questionable whether it is true, whether it is really love or an ego trip.

Stop for a moment, close your eyes, think of someone you love and say "I love you." How does it sound? And what do you think; is the "I" more important, or is the "you" more important? If it's the "I" that's being emphasized, chances are you're on an ego trip and that's when the other person can easily feel hurt. But if the "you" seems more important, that's not particularly wonderful either.

Two friends have to be equal. Obviously, since we're all different, two people don't bring the same thing to the table, but if one person feels more in love than the other, this creates problems. What really works is your egos falling away through this sense of intimacy.

To me love is intimacy. Intimacy does not mean *you* and *me*, it means that together we let go. Our egos dissolve because it feels so good just to be in bed together, just to have lunch together. Life is no longer a competition. It is enjoyment. It's beautiful when two people in love can drop their little egos just for a minute.

By the way, I don't want you to read this book and try to be enlightened all day long. I want you to breathe into each moment. When you are with your girlfriend and all of a sudden you just love her, you don't even want to tell her, because it is a bit embarrassing. But, when the personality falls away, you are just two people enjoying a loving space created by the temporary deaths of your two egos. That is a win-win situation.

I am an old friend of death. My birth mother died when I was one year old and left me with my fifteen-year-old sister-mother, who a few years later also left her body. She left me with Osho, who also left his body.

Death does not surprise me. Death has a look. Osho had that look. What surprises me is living. I can handle death, but I am still mangled by life and I must confess that aloneness rocks my world. Like most sannyasins who've been around for a while, I can quote Osho from both sides now. I am enlightened most of the time.

The only reason I am not leading Satsang at Starbucks today is because when aloneness speaks to me I shake from my core. I can't drink coffee without spilling my guts out. It's easy for Osho to say "Never born, never died," but where does that leave me while I am still here?

When Osho left his body, some of my female friends filled up the space of aloneness by getting pregnant. I know several kids with the name "India." I even met an "Osho." Good luck with that one, kiddo.

Many of my male friends went back into the marketplace and got busy with business. Think about it; how do you fill yourself up with when you feel such emptiness? Food? Sex? Relationships? Drugs? Another Master who is still alive? We are born alone, we die alone, and in the middle we do our best to stuff ourselves with…something. Maybe anything. Or everything.

For seventeen years I filled myself with a relationship. For seventeen years, I had a great partner who saved me from being alone. Her name is Jwala. "Jwala" means fire. We had an open relationship and, in the end, she left me for a younger version of me, making me experience death one more time.

I know what you are thinking: open relationships don't work. But how many monogamous relationships do you know that worked for seventeen years? It all depends on your perspective. Since all relationships end, maybe we should say that all relationships don't work. But the truth is that all relationships do work, for as long as you are together. They may work smoothly, they may work haphazardly, but they work.

At the very same time Jwala left me, my beloved niece Risa got cancer. Risa thinks of me as her brother, since when she was born, I had already been adopted by her mother, who was actually my sister.

Jwala leaving me was like drinking a triple espresso, and Risa getting the Big C was like adding two lumps of sugar-flavored cyanide. The combination was lethal. I fell apart. I died. My body grew old in a moment, my head felt chopped off, my heart burst, and I felt like I got kicked in the belly.

I remember Osho once saying in a discourse, "First I cut off your head, then I rip out your heart, then I kick you in the belly and finally, you remember who you are."

Please don't quote me on this, because I know these are not Osho's exact words. The way he expressed himself was more elegant. But that's what he said, more or less, and when I had that experience with Jwala and Risa I understood what he was talking about.

I was alone in the universe. In reality, I was lonely. All that I loved was in the past. Even on a rainy day, I wore sunglasses. The smile on my face was created by the fear that you would not love me if you knew about my pain. I sang to myself, paraphrasing Janis Joplin, *Aloneness is just another word for nothing left to lose.*

Sixty-seven years on this planet, 39 years with Osho and 17 with Jwala. When Jwala left me, I wept. She said, "I can't leave you if you are crying."

I said, "No, I am so happy you are in love with your new friend. I am only crying because I don't know how to be alone." Well, come to think of it, I wasn't *so* happy she was in love with another guy. To be honest, I'd like to have pushed him into one of Amsterdam's famous canals. But the bit about not knowing how to be alone was perfectly true.

I knew what Osho meant when he said that the ultimate question in life, when disillusionment and heartbreak hit you, is "Suicide or sannyas?" Jump off a cliff or jump into yourself?

But before you write me off as a poor excuse for a human being, think again, because I made it through to the other side of loneliness. I got it! I am home alone. How did I do it? I can't explain it, even to myself, at least not in a way that would make sense. Sometimes life just happens.

I think it had something to do with me finally accepting that I am alone. My family, my sister-mother, Osho, Jwala, Risa…they were never me in the first place. They were just dramas. For me, drama is when I am so involved in my own story that I think it is true and lose my inner sense of witnessing and watching – not to mention losing my sense of humor.

I always felt that Osho was hinting that it was a great idea for Krishna Prem to have his own head on his own shoulders and a bad idea when Krishna Prem had his head on Osho's shoulders. Simply said, I finally became the center of my very own cyclone.

Fast forward ten years to 2020, the year of the Great Global Pandemic. Jwala and I are still best friends. I am in Amsterdam rooming with her, just as friends, because she is still in love but now he is in America. He can't come here, so I can stay...for a while.

When we lie together, cuddling softly, I sometimes take a peek at her and whisper in her ear, "I don't want us back."

It's only partly true. On New Year's Eve, I said to her "Well, it is months since you have seen your boyfriend and months since I have played around with anyone. I just read a report that old lovers, if they get completely drunk, can rekindle their sexy story."

I swear to God I didn't make this up. This is a scientific study based on actual research and published in some psychology magazine.

Jwala laughed at me and said, "Great! It is New Year's Eve, so let's open a bottle of apple juice. I believe that report, but I am not interested to make love with you. Let's just have a drink and go back to sleep. Krishna, I have moved on."

It took me a while but then I laughed also. When we were a couple, we had an open relationship. Now that we are best friends, we never cheat on each other. Friendship is a higher value than a relationship...maybe.

A long time ago, I sent Osho a joke that I still love to this day. I sent him this joke forty years ago, so I am sure you must have heard it by now, but I don't know if you get the significance of it.

For me, a great joke is like reading the Bible, or maybe a joke has even more truth in it, because to be honest I never got the

Bible. I tried reading it. Maybe because I didn't love it, I never got it. I am fine without a Bible but I am not fine without a good joke. So here is the joke; it is simple:

Abby is a great man, very, very loving towards his wife, towards his community and towards his temple. Out of his abundance, he was always able to share and he did it all for God; every time he shared, he really was saying,

"Hey God, look at me, I am such a good man."

When he shared with the community, he always related everything he did in the world to his way of saying to God, "I love you."

One day, Abby was sitting in his home in Southern California, just relaxing in his living room, when he felt a rumble. He had been in earthquakes before, but this one felt stronger than usual. Soon, there was a knock on his door and he went to the front door; it was the fire department.

"Abby, there is going to be a tsunami today," warned the fire chief. "You have been so good to the community, we want to save you. Come with us."

"In my hour of need, only God can save me," Abby replied.

The fire chief couldn't believe him, but shrugged and replied, "Well, that is up to you. But we have other people in the neighborhood to evacuate, so I have to go now. Good luck."

The tsunami swept in from the coast and the water forced Abby to go up to the second floor of his house. Soon afterwards, the US Coast Guard arrived in a rescue boat.

"Come on, Abby," shouted the captain. "The tsunami is getting bigger every minute and we can save you."

"In my hour of need, only God can save me," Abby replied.

The water kept rising and Abby was forced to climb up on his roof, just as a US Air Force helicopter arrived.

"Abby, we have come to save you!" shouted the pilot.

"In my hour of need, only God can save me," Abby replied.

Finally the tsunami surged even higher, wrecked Abby's home and he drowned.

A short while later, Abby found himself in heaven, sitting in front of God, and he was totally pissed off. He would not even look at God.

God says, "Hi Abby! What's wrong? I've been waiting to see you. I want to thank you for all the good work you did on earth. But you seem very upset. What's going on?"

Abby replied, "God, after all I did for you, where were you in my hour of need? Where were you when the tsunami flooded my home and I was drowned? How come you didn't rescue me?"

God said, "What are you talking about? I sent the fire department, I sent the US Coast Guard, and I sent the US Air Force. I tried to save you, but you didn't listen to anybody!"

The moral of the story is that, well, here we are. The fire department is God, the Air Force is God. God is all around us in this life, and people like Abby are acting as if this life is not good enough because only God in heaven is good enough. A guy who believes in God is just as vulnerable to death as a person who doesn't believe in God. The moral of the story is to participate in life as if everything is divine – and to participate totally.

There's a beautiful response by Osho that I remember well. People used to come to him and ask, "Osho, is there an after-life?"

He would reply, "Never mind about the after-life. The question you need to ask yourself is, 'Is there a before-death life?' Because you are alive right now but you are not really living. Put your total energy into this life and then later on you can worry about the after-life."

So, don't worry about death. Death will come looking for you whenever it's your time and then there's nothing you can do except to say, "Hey dude, it would've been nice if you'd

showed up a little later, because I'm in the middle of a few issues that need taking care of, but okay, let's go."

By the way, there is this wonderful old Sufi story about a guy called Mustafa, who lived in a village near Baghdad. He was a servant to a rich man called Ali. One day, Mustafa went to the market place to buy some vegetables for his master and he saw Death standing there. Death looked at him and seemed to make a gesture towards him, so Mustafa dropped his vegetables and ran back to his master's house.

He told Ali what had happened and begged his master, "Please master, lend me your fastest horse so that I may leave this village and thereby escape my fate!"

"Where will go you?" asked Ali.

Mustafa said, "I will ride all the way to Al-Fallujah." This was the nearest big town to their little village, but many miles away. Ali gave his consent, gave Mustafa the horse, and watched his servant gallop off into the distance.

Ali became curious and walked down to the marketplace, where, indeed, he saw Death standing there.

Boldly, Ali approached Death and asked him, "Why did you make a hostile gesture towards my servant Mustafa?"

Death shook his head. "I made no hostile gesture," he replied. "I was surprised to see him here, for I have an appointment with him tonight, in Al-Fallujah."

Death cannot be escaped, but before that happens, we need to be sure to fully explore this life. This is an opportunity for experiencing what might be described as "before death living."

For me, exploring "before death living" is about taking care of myself. It is not about anyone else. And it is fun, because in meditation, we often use the word "discriminate," but it is not about the color of your skin, or the name of your religion. It is about discriminating between what is good for you and what is not good for you.

Sometimes you find out by throwing yourself into the fire — metaphorically speaking, I mean, like taking on a real challenge. Sometimes you watch the fire from a distance for a while and then decide, *Yes, I will pass through that fire because it looks like a good challenge for me.* Sometimes, too, you look at a fire and shake your head, *That looks really interesting and may be the right thing for some people, but I don't need to do that to myself.*

You learn from discriminating and you may still make mistakes, but you learn to make a mistake only once. It is interesting how they say in the East that an intelligent man does not make the same mistake twice. An intelligent man learns from any mistake he makes and moves on.

So, we are going to repeat in this book, that it's great to feel absolutely free to explore everything in life but try not to make the same mistake twice. That is the sign of an intelligent person. And if you keep making the same mistakes, my feeling is you should be running for public office, because those are the people who are determined not to look inside themselves.

Theoretically speaking, I guess it is possible for a politician or a pope to get to know their inner reality, but it's a one-in-a-million shot, because their whole focus is on seeking support from others, from outside themselves.

When you're busy projecting a popular public image and asking for votes, it's kinda hard to remember that lasting fulfillment is to be found only in your aloneness. You get my point? To a politician, image is everything. The inner world is nothing. You need votes, not a reminder of your own emptiness.

The nature of this book is to see who you are, not to see your face on an election billboard. That billboard face, like I said earlier, is made of plastic, because that's the kind of phony face you need in order to get elected and succeed in the marketplace of life.

That face has been created through years and years of not being yourself, years and years of responding to other people instead of yourself. To the point where one day you actually hate yourself so much, that you begin to hate the people that taught you how to be plastic.

But it was not their fault. The same thing was done to them and they have no idea there's an authentic face beneath the plastic one. That's the difference. Now you know what they could never have dreamed of knowing.

You know the truth. And the truth will set you free.

I don't know my name. I don't know your name either. But I do remember faces. So the next 4 pages are pictures of friends who held my hand during this writing journey... without their handles.

Come to think of it, I remember Vanesa Ramirez Crespo's name because she pulled this book out of me one word at a time. She then edited my words into book form. Full credit also goes to Anand Subhuti who edited my book to life as Vanesa is Spanish and I barely speak English. Subhuti is a master at making me look conscious...very hard work indeed! And special thanks to Anila Manning for proofreading. Anila was more like a therapist giving Subhuti's and my words a couple-counseling session. All together, my friends turned this book into a masterpiece…or should I say a disciplepiece.

My artwork was created Shanti Rowley. I asked Shanti to paint my vision board. And it came out so beautifully, I asked her if I could use it for my cover.

Last but not least, I want to thank the gals that got away… and remain my best friends even now. My beloveds Jwala and Yogini.

"Get out of your head and get into your heart. Think less feel more."

Osho

Chapter Nine

BE AN INDIVIDUAL

I give to my friend one bowl. Eat sweet and bitter, good and bad, consciousness, unconsciousness. Enjoy both and you will be nourished, and you will become very, very strong. And your strength will not be the opposite of softness, no.

The stronger you will be, the more fragile too. And this is beauty – when a strong man is fragile like a flower. Strong like a sword and fragile like a flower; then you are total. Then you are undivided, then you are indivisible, then you are really an individual. Individual means that which cannot be divided. You have come home, you have become one; now you can relax and rest. Osho

I remember what it is like to be innocent. I remember the very first time I held a girl's hand, feeling the warmth of her soft, delicate touch, and, even more astonishing to me, I felt the warmth of the girl's presence behind it, like she was communicating a silent "yes" to this unexpected intimacy between us. It was like a whole new world opening up before me.

Of course, I'd held hands with girls lots of times before…playing party games and that kind of stuff. After all, I had sisters. But this was different. This was holding hands in a very different way and even though I was just fourteen years old, a young, spotty teenager, I knew it had something to do with love.

She was older than me and the girlfriend of an older guy. There were five of us in all, out for an afternoon walk by the side of a lake when it started raining hard, so we ran for shelter into a small barn and stood close together, waiting for the shower to pass.

That's when she slipped her hand softly into mine, like a secret bond between us, and her boyfriend didn't even notice. But he was, after all, her boyfriend, so nothing happened beyond that brief, intense moment of sweetness and closeness. I still remember it today, precisely because it was innocent, fresh, unexpected…alive.

Innocence, for sure, is a relative phenomenon. Remember how the fantasy television series *Game of Thrones* came bursting into our living rooms in 2011? It knocked us back with its scenes of explicit nudity and horrendous visions of violence and death. But, curiously enough, one of the very first nude scenes portrayed a similar quality of innocence.

Remember? One of the less likeable characters, the exiled Prince Viserys Targaryen approaches his sister while she is in the bath and bids her come out so he can inspect her body.

She stands in full frontal nudity before him and he finds her suitable for his scheme to marry her off to the Dothraki warlord, Drogo, so he can ally himself with the powerful chieftain and regain his lost throne.

Prince Viserys is far from innocent. He lost that quality years ago, if he ever had it in the first place, and had likely been scheming and plotting for most of his life. But when his beautiful, blonde sister stands naked before him, she conveys something of that innocent quality we all have tasted.

She is no schemer. She is young, trusting and willing to do her brother's bidding. We cannot even begin to dream of her eventual destiny as a commander of dragons, ruler of people, and ultimately the destroyer of an entire city, King's Landing.

This kind of innocence is always lost, because it contains within itself a kind of ignorance. We're innocent because we're experiencing something for the first time and we don't know what's happening. Incidentally, that's what happened with LSD in the sixties and explains why it was such a revelation and wonder drug in the beginning and such a nightmare in the end.

It gave us a magical and colorful experience of innocence and a new way of looking at ourselves, as well as at nature and at love. But slowly the human mind got a grip on the trip, so to speak, and all was lost. The same is true of life in general. As we gather experience, our ignorance is replaced with knowledge and our innocence naturally disappears.

JC once commented, "Unless ye become as innocent as these little children, ye shall not enter my kingdom of heaven." But nobody can get back there, to childhood, so what did he mean? He was referring to a new kind of innocence, when we drop all knowledge and bring ourselves totally here and now, in this, the present moment.

We can live each moment as if it is a fresh, sparkling dewdrop, which in a way it really is. Every moment that is given to us is unique, pristine, fresh, and we need to be fully present to experience it with innocence.

After innocence comes enthusiasm. For example, at around the age of 28 it is very difficult to meditate. You are too much excited about life, you have so much energy; why would you pause to you ask yourself "Who am I?" Is that going to impress the girl you just met on Tinder, which, by the way, wasn't in existence when I was that age. Internet dating came way, way later.

But 28 can be a turning point — that's why I mention it. Ask an astrologer friend and she'll be happy to tell you. It's the time of your "Saturn Return," meaning that the planet Saturn returns to the position it had when you were born — it takes 28 years for Saturn to go around the sun.

This is the time when you can create a dramatic shift in personal values. Up to this time, you most likely followed the wishes and desires of your parents. For example, you went to university and got a Ph.D. in Biochemistry or French Medieval History and your parents were real proud of you, because none of their friends had kids who did that.

But then Saturn came knocking on your door and suddenly you got the feeling that all of that studying was just an incredible waste of time and energy. In moment of devastating revelation, you see everything is lying on the ground in front of you: your education, your career, your parents' dreams...everything has fallen.

By the way, if you ever want to see this moment on the silver screen you simply have to go and see *The Graduate*. I know, you've already seen it, but maybe not from such a profound perspective. It's really a great movie. Director Mike Nichols took a huge gamble on casting the unknown Dustin Hoffman for the main role, but it paid off spectacularly as Hoffman's portrayal of anti-hero Benjamin Braddock became a global sensation.

I just cannot move on from *The Graduate* without mentioning the line that went into everyone's Top 100 all-time favorite movie one-liners. Yes, of course, you know what I'm about to say: *plastics*. It's neat to remember it now, because we've just been talking about how plastic we all can be when we polish our personalities.

In the unlikely event that you've forgotten the context, Benjamin is attending a cocktail party thrown by his parents to celebrate his graduation, when a well-meaning friend of his father takes him outside and says, "I want to say one word to you (long pause)…plastics. There's a great future in plastics…."

It's a fabulously delivered line, illustrating the yawning gulf between an older man in business and a younger man in the business of becoming. That was a truly rebellious movie, released at a truly rebellious time: 1967 when the hippies were celebrating their "Summer of Love" and drugs, sex, and rock 'n roll promised to change the world.

But times change and, to be honest, I haven't seen a flicker of rebellion of any significance in any generation since the sixties. I don't know what happened. Everyone started to wake up and then they all went back to sleep. They can text each other, but they can't transform themselves.

That doesn't matter, because you, as the beautiful and courageous individual that you are, can wake up any time. And one thing that's going to happen, when you step away from the seductive dreams manufactured by society, is that you're going to find yourself standing like Daenerys Targaryen outside her bathtub: naked, vulnerable, and very much alive.

Before that moment arrived, existence, youth and a shot of hormones gave us too much energy to pay attention to ourselves. We were so busy growing up and exploring the world, which, by the way, looked pretty exciting and attractive...right up until that moment when we hit the wall. Right up until Saturn breathed on the back of our necks and we suddenly saw the proverbial rat race for what it was, and then first we scratched our heads, then we shook those very same heads in an emphatic "no thanks."

So, the essence of this book is that, once you hit the wall, you can transform yourself, take off the plastic smile from your plastic face, and actually go forward as a newly awakened — or maybe newly awakening — human being.

Also, you might, without picking up the plastic, return to being a lawyer, or a social worker, or a businessman, or whatever occupation you were in, but now you know it's not the real deal. You might return to taking care of your family, but now you know, it's okay to secretly giggle at the role you've chosen to play.

You can't give out your natural smile with a plastic face on. We are not talking about plastic surgery here; we are talking about dropping the plastic personality that would have carried you further and further into the American Dream and you wouldn't have even noticed when the dream became a nightmare.

Fortunately, you remembered Benjamin Braddock just in time and, avoiding the extra effort involved in making love with Mrs. Robinson, decided to take off the plastic before it became permanently glued to your body. And that is when the watching consciousness is born and you look down at all that plastic on the floor. That is my version of joy, when you look at the plastic and laugh.

For every person that laughs there are a million people who, when they hit a wall, gather up the plastic pieces, put them in a plastic bag, bring it to a plastic surgeon and ask, "Hey, can you put me back together please?"

This reminds me of Jake Sully. Forgive me but this chapter seems to be about movie metaphors. Do you need me to remind you who Sully was? Really? Has it been so long since James Cameron wowed the movie world with his epic, 3D, science-fiction blockbuster *Avatar*?

Jake Sully, you will now recall, was an injured, paraplegic Marine who volunteers for an experiment on Planet Pandora, where he discovers the joy of being whole and healthy in the form of a native avatar. He falls so much in love with his new avatar self and with the planet and its tribes that he no longer wants to be human, or work for the mining company that's threatening the planet.

It's a great metaphor: when we are fully alive and in tune with our own energy and the natural wonder of our planet, we can also feel like avatars, even without the need to change bodies. But when we sacrifice our humanity and our life energy for the sake of making a buck, or playing it safe, we are just cripples, mere shadows of who we have the potential to be.

Cameron's movie carried a distinctive anti-corporate, anti-business message, which is truly ironic because although it cost a staggering $237 million to make the film, it grossed an almost unbelievable $2.8 billion at the box office. And who benefited from those profits? Of course, the corporations that financed it.

By the way, in case you're wondering, I'm neither anti-corporate nor anti-business, although I'm sure that sometimes I sound like it. It's just that life is so short and so precious it seems crazy to get a full-time job and spend so much time in an office making a buck.

And another thing: it's interesting to see how popular these kinds of movies are, in which the hero or heroine breaks out from the straitjacket of mainstream values and discovers a new kind of freedom. Millions of people vicariously enjoy the exhilaration of liberation…and then what? They leave the cinema and go back to living their conventional lifestyle, as if it had been only a dream on the screen, not an invitation for emancipation.

Okay, enough of movies. You get the picture, right? The opportunity we all have is to liberate, to celebrate, to understand that this life-affirmative vision can be shared by everyone. It's not a case of limited supply. It's not an "either me or you" kind of deal. In fact, it gets even better when I realize that I am happier when you are also happy – we can go higher and deeper together, along with the whole goddamned planet.

When I am excited, there is room for you to be excited. It is not a competition. When I am ecstatic, there is room for you to be ecstatic. So, I am not writing this book for the people who want to pay a visit a plastic surgeon.

I am writing this book for the person who is saying, "Finally, I have come to a point where I am alone and I am alive. Let's go have meditation with Krishna Prem and enjoy ourselves."

So, this book is for a very few people. If by chance this book becomes a bestseller, then it was a lousy book. We are writing this book for about one percent of people in the whole world. The one percent who can say, "My God, being miserable is not enough!"

There is room in this world to fly and this is what my teacher Osho called Zorba the Buddha. He was a buddha and he loved the fictional character Zorba the Greek, created by

Nikos Kazantzakis, because of his zest for life. He wanted me to become a Zorba because this approach to life releases so much energy, and he knew this energy would be needed for the next step of becoming a buddha.

In fact, meditation requires just as much energy as the effort, say, of becoming President of the United States. Osho was encouraging us to put the same amount of energy *into not becoming President*. He wanted us to put that same energy into meditation and awareness.

He would say, "The best buddhas were originally Zorbas," precisely because it requires a lot of energy to make the jump into your own buddhahood. And Zorba has that energy in spades, as they say. But you may object: "Hey Krishna, if being Zorba is so great, why should I bother to switch to being a buddha?"

A very good question, my friend, but consider this: The problem with being a fabulous Zorba is that, if you get too much identified with it, you think you are going to be young and beautiful and exciting for your whole life. It ain't the case. Sooner or later, as the great clock of life goes on ticking, your energy will start to fade, and then you will regret not adding buddha to your soul while you were still bursting with the juice of life.

With this in mind, I hope you understand that I am not interested in coming to you from a space of meditation. I am not a deeply spiritual, holy-moly kinda guy. I am interested in being totally in the world and encouraging everyone else to do the same, to the point where it's possible for anyone to say, "It's been fun and what else is new?"

Then meditation happens. Do you know what I mean? It is very interesting. You might come to this point after a successful marriage, after a career as a lawyer, after – or maybe during – the time of raising your kids, but now it is real and you are ready to change. This book is about the quality of that experience.

I always love when Osho said, "Pray like a lover, not like a beggar." For example, whenever you finish making love, after you enjoyed your orgasm and you are relaxed, you can discover this is a great time to pray because you are so satisfied right now. Then you're not nagging God, asking "Give me this... give me that...." You're communing with him in a state of gratitude and fulfillment. I know, this is not what they taught you in Sunday school, but hey, looking back, can you seriously believe that your Sunday school teacher knew anything about prayer?

Zorba rocks. Without sex, you might not know how exciting life can be. Without dancing, you might never know how exciting life can be. And the reason we get mad at ourselves is that we know dancing is ecstatic, we know that making love creates a state of prayer in us, but we're so goddamned tired when we get home from work that we don't have the energy for any of it.

How many of you are working eight or ten hours a day and not enjoying that work? Because if you ever want to get to that point of liberating yourself you need to find a job that doesn't drain your energy, so you can make a few bucks without feeling it sucks.

Love the work you do, or do the work you love. When you watch yourself and you love what you do, time disappears. If you watch yourself and don't love what you do, time gets very long and exhausting.

I can guarantee that if you haven't been meditating so far in your life, it's because you have been doing something that somebody else felt was a great idea. For example, you got this current job because somebody else told you it would be a good job for you. But it's not really you and that's why you're tired instead of joyful.

First, you need ask yourself who you are, then you can do something you love. That doubles the energy and the name of the game is that we are trying to get juicy. This the basic idea: how to be more juicy.

When I first heard Osho say, "Squeeze the juice from life!" I didn't hear him right. I thought he said, "Squeeze the Jews from life!" and every night for a week I had nightmare flashbacks of my ethnic history.

No, I'm kidding. I heard him right and that's why I love him, because any ethnic background will do, and anyway sooner or later on the path of meditation you're going to disidentify with all of it. Meditation is for everyone and squeezing the juice from life is something we can all learn.

We just need to discover our life energy and our passion for living every moment with totality. Like, for instance, right now. Okay?

Chapter Ten
YOU HAVE COME HOME

If your awareness lacks love then it is still impure. It has not yet known one hundred percent purity. It is not yet really awareness. It must be mixed with unawareness. It is not pure light. There must be pockets of darkness inside you still working, functioning, influencing you, dominating you. If your love is without awareness, then it is not love yet. It must be something lower, something closer to lust than to prayer.

So let it be a criterion if you follow the path of awareness, let love be the criterion. When your awareness suddenly blooms into love, know perfectly well that awareness has happened, samadhi has been achieved. If you follow the path of love, then let awareness function as a criterion, as a touchstone. When suddenly, from nowhere, at the very center of your love, a flame of awareness starts arising, know perfectly well...rejoice! You have come home. Osho

I came from a teaching called monogamy. And I totally found out that unless it comes from my heart, monogamy is a prison. Nowadays, young people are coming from a great deal more freedom, but freedom without love is also a prison.

So, we need freedom and love. My generation came from monogamy and it didn't work, The next generation is going to come from playing around on the dating apps but, in the end, both don't work until you add the missing X-factor.

In other words, it is fine to lead your life any way you want, but if you don't bump into love then it's better to ask for forgiveness from your partner and move on.

Freedom with love is ecstasy, pure ecstasy. So, please don't tell me how many women you have slept with, how many guys you have played with. Tell me how many times you have been in love, and I'm sure you will remember that it feels a whole lot better than casual sex.

Nature needs sex and so do we. That's how the dance of life keeps on dancing, from the tango to the fandango — not to mention the *paso doble*, which I can't even pronounce, let alone learn those steamy bull-fighting dance steps. So, don't misunderstand me, there's nothing wrong with exploring sex and enjoying sex. Especially when you are young, curious and bursting with hormones. That's the right time to explore.

Sex is the foundation on which the temple of love can be built. Without it, you may still build a temple but it's not going to feel very alive and attractive to hang out there. It's just that as you grow older, you get to value love more and sex less.

Let me ask you: if you slept with one thousand women and never met love, or if you made love to one woman and you fell in love, which is better? Hmm, that's a tough call for a sexy guy, right? Love is always better, but when I say that, I'm coming from the place of a guy who, as far as sex is concerned, has filled up his quota. If you'd asked me the same question 30 or 40 years ago, I may have given a different answer.

Anyway, the good news is: we don't have to choose. We can explore sex and we can trust that love will come our way if we stay open and receptive. And if we don't put love in a jail called marriage, then love combined with freedom is even better – more risky, for sure, but worth the risk because then we might find ourselves experiencing ecstasy.

Ecstasy. These days, it's the name of a drug as well as a natural human state of...well, ecstasy...so let's break the law for a moment and look from the perspective that we are all drug addicts: sex is a drug, love is a drug, and ecstasy is the ultimate drug.

Ecstasy overwhelms you, dissolves you, and disappears you. Unfortunately, ecstasy also knows there is such a thing called agony – and that's no fun at all. It may be character- building and transforming, but, as you surely know, it ain't no Sunday afternoon picnic in the park.

Maybe you bump into ecstasy because you have lived in agony. You have explored the territory of extreme *angst* and you have learned your lesson and turned inwards toward meditation and awareness for a solution.

Ecstasy does not bubble up inside you without awareness, because meditation and awareness are needed to keep open those secret, mysterious, inner doors through which ecstasy can rise up and flood your being. So, again, do whatever you want but make sure you bring awareness along with you in your back pocket.

Tantra is the art of bringing awareness with you while you are making love. These days, however, the word "Tantra" tends to be an over-used expression — Tantra can mean anything from good sex to oh-my-god sex — so it seems safer to stick with awareness. By which I mean, the consciousness inside you that is capable of watching and witnessing everything you do, think, say, or feel.

Awareness allows you to see how you treat the other person. It allows you to focus more on sensitivity and subtle energy flow, less on doing push-ups. But, on the other hand, if push-ups are what's happening and it feels good, then awareness helps you bring even more focus to this vigorous form of sexual gymnastics.

At first, it's not so easy to watch while you are having an orgasm, but, speaking from personal experience, after a while, you can do even that. It takes time for the witness to convince the body that it has far more capacity for sensation than its owner ever realized.

Osho created a beautiful technique to experience...no, not sex. It's not a Tantric technique. It's a method for emptying and cleaning the mind called, appropriately enough, *No Mind*. It's also called *Gibberish*, just throwing out the garbage in your mind.

Now, you know me, I jump all over the place because I write the way I think. So, why would I be thinking of doing a meditation method called No Mind when I'm talking about making love? The answer is that if you really want to bring your total energy to the act of love- making, then it's a good idea to empty your mind first.

I love my mind. No, really, I do. It's a fun machine and useful when you're trying to learn how to install a dating app such as Tinder, Bumble, OkCupid, Match, Grindr, or — love this one —

Coffee Meets Bagel. Just think, somewhere on this amazing planet, there is a Bagel waiting to dunk itself in my Coffee…. wow! How cool is that?

But you surely must have noticed that your mind, like my mind, is full of unnecessary crap. I mean, you're just about to kiss an attractive woman for the first time and then, wouldn't you know, your mind starts flashing images of your previous relationship, or of a mass shooting you just saw on the six o'clock news, or it suddenly wants to know why Albert Einstein thinks that energy equals mass times a constant….

You catch my drift? There's a lot of extra stuff going on, with images passing by like cars on a highway, because the unconscious part of your mind is vast and crammed with every image you ever saw, whether on TV or in real life. It's a junkyard filled with madness. We need to become good friends with our own madness and unload some of it, right now, so that's when we start thinking about No Mind Meditation and doing gibberish.

By the way, a minor diversion here: according to Osho, the word "gibberish" comes from a Sufi mystic called Jabbar, who never spoke a proper language. Seeing the superficial bullshit of normal communication, he chose to convey his spiritual message by talking only nonsense. And another thing about Jabbar, totally unrelated, is that clocks and watches stopped whenever he came near them. So, no time, no mind…and therefore no problem.

Did Jabbar really exist? Well, let me say that Osho was never too bothered about facts and he never referred to notes while giving his discourses. When trying to make a point, he just grabbed hold of whatever information came into his head at the time and conveyed it to us as the Absolute Truth. So Jabbar could have been a figment of his own creative imagination.

But then again, maybe not. This elusive mystic might have been Osho's customized version of Jebir Ibn Hayyad, an Arab alchemist in the ninth century, who wrote so many treatises on so many subjects that no one could be sure if what he was saying was true or not.

So, what do I mean, when I say that you should start doing gibberish? I mean you sit down, close your eyes, and — preferably accompanied by a few other crazy meditators — you start talking nonsense, as loudly and as energetically as possible, accompanied by any kind of gesture or facial expression you like.

It's a bit like the second stage of Dynamic Meditation, but the difference here is that you don't scream, beat pillows, cry, etc. You pour your energy into the nonsense sounds you are making. You can shout it, you can whisper it, you can maybe even giggle it, but you keep on speaking nonsense. Like Osho says about the No Mind method: "Speak any language you don't understand."

By the way, Osho structured this meditation as follows: half an hour of gibberish and half an hour of total silence. Its purpose: to empty the mind so you can experience what it's like to have silence inside your head.

Now, when you go on a dating website, you want to tell the potential candidates that you are good looking, warm, friendly, that you have a good job, and have just been too busy to meet the right person. Certainly, you are not going to go on a dating site and start doing gibberish, "Blah, blah, blah, blah, blah...."

You want to present yourself in a way that ensures that people like you and at the same time you're hoping to meet a person whom you like. You ignore the fact that you are not presenting an honest picture of who you really are, so most probably the person you are meeting isn't willing to show you who they really are either.

Maybe that's okay because maybe the only thing you both want is a one-night stand. But most people are hoping for more. So, what usually happens is that we meet for the first time as who we are not, and then slowly start to get real as we continue seeing each other.

It's unlikely that you're going to go on a dating site and openly admit, "I feel really scared of who I actually am. So, let's get real." Okay, there's a million-to-one chance that if you did, you might actually meet somebody else who is also ready to admit that she is scared, wants to be real, and is open to hooking up with you. But otherwise, it's a slow process of gradually building trust and taking off the plastic masks.

One function of the No Mind Meditation is to be a kind of pre-dating preparation — mental foreplay if you like — to clear out the junk. It's not just about paving the way for sex, love, and meeting Miss Universe. It's a baseline method for experiencing your life in a fresh and more sensitive way, because it means that your mind is taking a break from its endless habit of thinking...thinking...and thinking. About what? About anything.

Have you ever "thought" about it? Mind is a thought-producing factory. It exists to think. It doesn't really care about *what* you are thinking. As long as you keep on thinking your mind is happy. Weird, isn't it? But that's the way it is.

No Mind changes the gestalt. It invites the mind to discharge its load without thinking rationally and logically. In this way, it paves the way for you to be ready to fall in love. It clears the theater stage of props from previous dramas and invites a new romantic play to be performed.

So, when you meet Miss New, who you hope is going to be Miss Right, and maybe even Miss Forever, you come to this moment with a more relaxed and fresh attitude. Even if you are meeting Miss Oh-It's-You-Again, the encounter will seem new and revitalized.

You want to fall in love...or do you? Most of us come from our minds when we meet somebody. And one thing about our minds, which I'm sure you've noticed, is that they are never short of opinions, so they very soon tell us whether this person standing in front of us is the right one for us.

However, here's Catch 22: the person who we really are is not to be found in our minds, but in our bellies, in our guts, so it's hardly surprising if we end up making a mistake – the same mistake, usually, because we tend to follow a repeating pattern – and find ourselves dining out on a familiar recipe for disappointment.

I don't want to fall in love. I prefer to rise in love and, yes, this is possible for everyone. If I am comfortable being who I am – who I *really* am, I mean – and if I then meet someone who is comfortable with being who she is, then we can rise in love.

Rising in love is wonderful. Finding a lovely partner is so delightful that we can easily drift off into La-La-Land and fantasize, because everybody wants to meet, melt and merge with a Tantric partner, like the ones they show in advertisements for intimate and sensual weekend retreats: a god and goddess entwined in artistic, orgasmic embrace.

Meanwhile, let's keep our feet on the ground and, when we do meet each other, check out who we actually are and if we're a good fit. Initially, we might fall in love while getting horny and happy, then we might rise in love enough to disappear together during orgasm.

If you find that you want to share more than sex with that person, then rising in love is a possibility. If you just want to make love, you might need to lower your sights and accept that this connection might not be satisfying for the two of you for very long.

We are looking for the balance between being attracted to another person and whether that person can also meet us where we so badly want to be met, in a deeper way. This is where the importance of establishing a meaningful connection takes precedence over everything else on our boy-meets-girl agenda. In other words, we are not looking for codependency, security, safety, a wife or a husband, or even, at the opposite end of the spectrum, for a casual fuck- buddy.

We are two mature people who want to experience meeting each other with no conditions and with everything wide open. It is risky, because two mature people don't necessarily need to get married, nor immediately sign a contract for monogamy and a promise that "you will never sleep with anybody but me."

I'm not saying it's easy, but if you want to keep love alive then freedom is a must. You just have to keep walking into the unknown and the unpredictable.

I remember one time I was at a New England clambake and happened to find myself talking with a group of attractive women in their thirties. It was not a flirting situation because I knew they were all married and their husbands were standing together nearby, probably talking about cars or fishing.

Anyway, just for fun, I said to them, "It seems you are all happily married but have you ever thought of freeing up your marriage and experimenting with an open relationship?"

They didn't hesitate for a second. One after another, they all shook their heads. Then one of them said, "No, I could never do that, because I couldn't handle my jealousy!"

I thought that was interesting...a very humble approach. She wasn't saying "If my husband cheats on me I'll kill him!" or "Keep that bitch away from my man!" In fact, it wasn't the idea of her husband making love to another woman that was so daunting. It was knowing how much pain she herself would suffer and just how horrible the feeling of jealousy can be. She knew her limits and it was humble enough to acknowledge it.

I don't know if it's easier for men. Somehow, I doubt it. Nevertheless, I'm coming from a different space than this married woman. I like different flavors of ice cream, knowing that eventually I always come back to the flavor that I like the most.

Hopefully, that flavor is the woman I love and with whom I have a long-term open relationship, but the risk is always there that she'll be gone when I come back.

For me, monogamy is also okay, as long as it comes out of love. If it comes out of fear, I am not that impressed. Monogamy usually deteriorates into monotony, although few people will ever admit it.

One time in Amsterdam I was having breakfast with five male friends — each one from a different country — and every man was complaining about his wife. Every single one. At the end of the breakfast, I said, "Okay, let's put all our keys on the table."

Everybody put his bunch of keys on a table and I ordered five espressos. Then I said, "Let's agree that these keys are symbolic and they represent our relationship problems. Breakfast is over and now we have to go back to our daily lives and our daily wives. So I want you to pick up the problem that you like the most."

Every single man picked up his own keys. Every man is moaning about his wife but that is the problem he is choosing, the problem he prefers, which means he has accepted things as they are and isn't interested in changing the situation. He complains, but he is talking to his psychotherapist instead of talking to his wife.

I think many codependent people are actually in love with each other, but just do not know how to use the sword of awareness to improve their lives. The man is so afraid to be honest, he thinks his wife will run away, or maybe vice versa. He doesn't consider the possibility that it might be fun to grow up together.

Even if you have been married for 25 years, if you bring meditation into the relationship, everything can change. It might be scary, because the outcome might be you realize you are not suited for each other. But, on the other hand, you may discover you are even more in love than you realized. My experience has always been that people are married for a purpose.

However, I wouldn't write that book myself. That is up to you; I just think people actually like each other a lot more than they are prepared to admit. So, at the end of this book, maybe I will ask: "Would you want my wife or your wife? Do you want your keys or my keys?" I have never seen a man pick up another set of keys.

All this talk of husbands and wives reminds me of a true story that happened in California, just north of San Francisco on Highway 101. A guy was driving from Sausalito to Novato when he saw the blue flashing lights of a highway patrol car in his rear-view mirror. He realized he'd been speeding and was about to be booked.

He pulled over and the police car parked behind him. The officer got out, walked up to his window, leaned in and said, "Do you know you were speeding?"

The guy looked apologetic. "Yes, officer," he replied. "You see, a few days ago my wife suddenly disappeared. I reported to the police that she was missing and when I saw you in my mirror I was afraid you were bringing her back!"

The gag worked its magic. The cop laughed and let him off. No ticket.

Chapter Eleven

ABSOLUTE FREEDOM

The capacity to be alone is the capacity to love. It may look paradoxical to you, but it's not. It is an existential truth: only those people who are capable of being alone are capable of love, of sharing, of going into the deepest core of another person – without possessing the other, without becoming dependent on the other, without reducing the other to a thing, and without becoming addicted to the other. They allow the other absolute freedom, because they know that if the other leaves, they will be as happy as they are now. Their happiness cannot be taken by the other, because it is not given by the other. Osho

This book is about meditation, but my feeling is that many people reading this book are doing so because they are working with a therapist. If therapy is working well for you, that's terrific. My feeling is therapy can be even more effective if your therapist is a meditator and, actually, it works best of all when he happens to be a meditator and a friend.

Oftentimes, you see on TV soaps and reality shows how people are in therapy for fifteen or twenty years, but because they haven't yet discovered their inner witness they can't cut away the roots of their problems. It makes sense, right? I mean, you can't cut away a problem unless you are aware of its roots.

This is what meditation means: "I am aware of what I need to focus on as a way of working on in my life." The beauty is that as soon as I am aware of a specific problem, the problem has a way of disappearing. Not that the challenges of life disappear, but they are no longer seen in the context of problems to worry about.

By the way, if you start to feel that you miss your problems, don't worry. There are so many things in life that can be viewed as problems, you can always pick up another one. Some people feel uneasy without problems to chew on. Others get addicted to using the sword of their own awareness to cut away their problems and enjoy it so much they don't want to stop. So, be careful! Make sure you don't create problems just so you can use the sword of awareness. Okay, I'm kidding a little bit here, but the point is it feels good to be healthy and not weighed down by what you think are serious problems, when in fact there's no need to worry.

I want to point out that, for me, awareness is not the end of the search but the beginning
– simply a baby step. It means you are at home in yourself and you are consciously awake. You have cleaned up your basement and your attic, and you are no longer divided.

For example, as a man I tend to be attracted to female partners who are comfortably "at home" in their bodies. Why? Because even though I talk about meditation, I tend to spend a lot of time in my head, occupied by thoughts and ideas, which means that I'm not always grounded in my body, not always connected to the earth beneath my feet.

I love women who are comfortable in their bodies, whether they are doing yoga stretches or dance workouts, because they help to ground me, introducing me to my own body. In a nutshell, I like women who are comfortable in their bodies because I don't feel comfortable in mine, so I'm looking for that kind of reconnection.

It took me a while to fall in love with my own body instead of the body of the woman in bed beside me. It took time for me to see how the woman was just a mirror for what I was looking for in myself.

This is a good meditation exercise: look at your partner and see which of her natural qualities is attracting you and what it is that you hope to complete in yourself through being with her. If you can take responsibility for those missing qualities then you can begin to develop them in yourself and find your way to embrace wholeness.

In relation to what I've just been saying, I noticed, after a while, that the women I dated were always better looking than me. It was an interesting insight: I had to be with a good- looking woman so that people would think of me as a good-looking man, which I secretly doubted. Of course, that puts a lot of pressure on the woman and no pressure on myself, until I wake up to what I'm doing both to her and to me.

So, life for me is the big picture. Nike's slogan says, "Just Do It." It's the ultimate American sound bite. Just do it and get a great job. Just do it and find the right woman. Just do it and become President of the United States. Just do it and win the lottery. Just do it and become rich.

Just be rich! Well, there's no harm in adding a few extra bucks to your bank balance, but if it takes up all your time and makes you chronically stressed and anxious then you may want to re-evaluate.

For example, if you play the stock market, you may find yourself continuously preoccupied by the price of your shares as they rise and fall. Some folks can relax while playing that game, which impresses the hell out of me, but for others it wrecks their peace of mind.

Remember the end of the nineties, when computer technology made it feasible for ordinary folks to become day traders on the stock market? Suddenly, trading centers were opening up all over America and inviting what the *Washington Post* described as "the adrenaline-addicted, thrill-seeking cowboys of the electronic range."

Under-trained and over-enthusiastic, with high expectations, many of these day traders stayed glued to their computer screens all day, feverishly trying to guess which way the stocks were going to move and betting large sums on the outcome.

Then one fine day, an ordinary-looking guy who was day trading in Atlanta walked into the trading center, pulled out a gun and started shooting his colleagues. Then he shot his family and himself. According to newspaper reports he'd racked up more than $100,000 in losses and couldn't trade his way out of a downward spiral.

That's an extreme example of our hunger for riches. But for me, the wealthiest person isn't necessarily someone who has mastered the Tao of the Dow. He's someone who is committed to going all the way in an exploration of who he is inside. Anyone can go on this inner journey and it's free! Then you feel rich for who you are, not merely because you happen to have a lot of money.

In case you're wondering, I'm not against being rich. No way, José! But I'm looking for an energy flow between having money and the experience of feeling inner richness no matter how many zeros you have on your bank statement.

By the way, if you do have money and it still doesn't make you feel rich, then you can rest assured that you are spending too much time with cash and not enough time with yourself. Money is a convenient means of exchange that elevates us above the level of primitive barter societies. But there's a downside: money can become the be-all and end-all of existence and, sadly, there's never been a time in history when people are more crazy for money than they are today.

Remember the real estate bubble that burst in 2008? Repeated warnings from economic experts were brushed aside as bank chiefs who really should have known better kept buying mortgage derivatives worth essentially nothing, or "dog shit" as one insider called them.

Incidentally, that's a direct quote from a fascinating movie called *The Big Short*, about a few guys who made fortunes by betting against the realty market. What did they do that when everyone else didn't? Simple: they actually looked at the information inside the derivatives — instead of just buying them blindly — and understood they were worthless.

"Do the math," urged one exasperated schoolteacher as the bubble exploded, but in the surreal world of the US real estate market two plus two no longer equaled four. It was five, six or even six million — any number you cared to name. When house prices slumped and the bubble finally burst, millions of Americans felt the pain.

What was it that fueled this madness, turning even experienced financiers into idiots? Greed, my friend. Greed and the human mind's tendency to want more and more and more.... More of what? More of pretty much anything that glitters like gold.

We have been listening to our minds forever. Your mind has become your boss. I can confidently make this assertion even without knowing you, because it's a universal human condition. This amazing biological machine in our heads that helped us rise above the other animals to dominate the planet has also seized control of its owners and is taking us all for a ride.

I've never been very impressed with Stanley Kubrick as a movie director, but one movie that knocked my socks off was...yes...you know it already...*2001: A Space Odyssey*. The special effects were great, for 1968, and everyone remembers the Pan American spaceliner approaching the rotating space station to the tune of Johann Strauss' *Blue Danube* waltz.

The story was, well, kinda weird, and Kubrick deliberately fashioned it that way to keep us scratching our heads. I mean, any movie that ends with a foetus floating through space instead of being safely in his mother's tummy is basically bizarre.

As for Pan American, well, as all know, the one-time biggest and most prestigious international airline crash landed in 1991 and went bankrupt, a full decade before the year in which the space odyssey was supposed to happen.

But what I loved about *Space Odyssey*, as a metaphor, occurred during the space flight to Jupiter when HAL, the ship's sentient computer, decided to take over and eliminate the space crew, because he deemed the mission too important to be left in the hands of mere humans.

There you have it. That's what our minds have done to us. They've taken control of our lives because they think life is too important to be handled otherwise. In the movie, HAL's bid for control of the spaceship fails and his super-intelligent processor core is deactivated. But in real life HAL is alive and well, sitting inside our heads and running the show.

So the question here is: who is the boss, you or your mind? And when I say "your mind" that's not really accurate, because "your" mind isn't really yours. It has been created by the society surrounding you, so even though you think that it's your religion, your nation, your culture, in fact it's all been programmed into you by the society into which you happened to be born.

We are constantly giving up our power to others because we have forgotten to ask ourselves "Who am I?" Rather, we ask everybody else, "By the way, please tell me, who am I?" Or else you pull out your driver's license from your pocket, look at the photo, the name and address and reassure yourself, "Okay, that must be who I am, because if it's good enough for the State of California then it's good enough for me."

When is the last time you asked yourself the question "Who am I?" This the problem. This your dark night of the soul, even though the street lights are on outside your window and, practically speaking, your room isn't especially dark. It's darker inside yourself and as the late, great Leonard Cohen said shortly before shedding his mortal coil, "You want it darker."

In other words, if you ever want to find the true answer to "Who am I?" then you need to look inside and be okay with not getting the answer that makes you happy, right away.

You need to cut away all those moments, all those hundreds of moments in this lifetime, where you have been unreal. Not that you literally need to go through them all, one by one, making a long list of all your unconscious moments, meditating over each one and ticking it off. That would take forever and even then, chances are you'd miss the most important ones because you conveniently forgot about them.

All you really need to do is take a deep breath, exhale slowly and take full responsibility for everything that's happened in your life and for the way you've turned out as a human being. You take responsibility for the fact that you've been seduced by society, even though the process began when you were a tiny baby and you really didn't have any choice.

You take responsibility for the fact that you're in a spaceship run by a computer called HAL. Only, in our case, we're all traveling together in a spaceship called Planet Earth and it's a little more difficult to find the central core of the computer system because actually it's nothing but a bunch of collectively-held ideas that are passed from head to head.

Sure, you can locate your own personal bio-computer easily enough, but you don't want to deactivate that because then you'd become a brain-dead zombie and that's no fun at all. They used to do that, in the early days of brain surgery, back in the 1940s and 50s, especially to women who were deemed to be mentally disturbed.

It was an invasive form of psychosurgery called a lobotomy, a procedure severing the link between the two frontal lobes and the rest of the brain. Even at the time, it generated intense controversy, but many considered it to be a marvelous advance in medicine and one Portuguese pioneer even won a Nobel Prize for it.

Thousands of people were given lobotomies, especially in the USA and UK. Only later was it seen as a form of medical barbarism, trampling on the rights of those poor patients who were compelled to receive it.

No, let's not deactivate the brain. Rather, let's focus on the ideas that have been fed into your bio-computer and, even more importantly, on your attachment to those ideas – passed down to you by your mom and dad and all the others. In a cosmic nutshell:

HAL is not your bio-computer. HAL is your mind. HAL is not the container. HAL is the content.

By the way, your girlfriend or boyfriend is in the same boat, we're all in the same boat, so there's not going to be much help from outside yourself. You are going to have to do this alone. But once you are free the chances are you will turn to the significant other in your life – be it man, woman, or your pet dog – and say, "Hey, I actually like you!"

That is what you find out. This the cosmic joke, that once you become free, you find out that you want to say to your parents, "Thank you!" You want to turn to your wife or husband and say, "I am really sorry I had to put you through this, I had a feeling that we actually liked each other. I just didn't have the courage to say, 'Can we be naked together? Can we go through this life asking ourselves real questions about real life?'"

If we can do that, together, I think it can be a win-win: when I love myself so much that I give you space for you to fall in love with yourself. And that is to me, what relating is about; two conscious people saying, "Thank you, it is so nice to have a friend." And, by the way, once you bump into friendship, you are most likely going to bounce back into misery a few times.

It is not the easiest journey. It's more like a roller-coaster ride with spectacular ups and downs. You don't just go into the dark night of the soul, come out into bright sunlight on the other side and become free. Freedom can be a lonely affair. Many times you will say to yourself, *Shit, what did I get myself into? I want to get back to my comfortable, familiar attachments and all those people who need me to be the way I was before.* It takes courage to be free and to say "Thank you."

One evening recently I gave a talk to a group of young people. It really was a young audience. The oldest person in the audience was twenty-seven years old. They were all into meditation so they asked me to give them a talk about meditation. But they were in for a surprise because I basically said:

"I can talk for hours but you will not get what I am talking about. Because you are so young, you are so full of juice, that you can't possibly know what meditation is."

That may not be true, but it shocked them and I felt I had a valid point to make. Let me put it this way: when I was a hippie, before I met meditation, I used to agree with Timothy

Leary and say, "Never trust anybody over 30." Why? Because those generations all seemed to be so straight and conventional that I felt it was a recipe for suicide.

Now that I have "matured" and am more than twice 30, I have come to the conclusion that I don't trust anybody *under* 30 – not because I don't like them, but because they have so much energy there's not much chance they can sit still, close their eyes, and relax long enough to discover their own inner, witnessing consciousness. They have too much life juice bouncing up and down inside them and spilling out all over the place.

Sometimes, when I'm in India, I talk to kids on the road who are moving around the backpack circuit and checking out the spiritual scene: getting hugged by Amma, sitting in Satsang with Mooji, working in Sadguru's ashram, signing up for a yoga course in Rishikesh…and so on. One of the stops on their route is a ten-day Vipassana retreat with the Goenka people, who have centers all over India where you can do it for the price of a donation.

The interesting thing is that when these kids tell me about "doing Vipassana" it's like a challenge they have to meet in order to feel okay with their peers. Back in Tel Aviv or Berlin, they'll be at a friend's birthday party or at a dance and say, "Yeah, sure, I sat for ten days in Vipassana and did nothing!" Very cool.

This reminds me of *Into the Wild,* a movie about a young American guy who liked to challenge himself in extreme situations. He had a lot of courage and did a lot of crazy stuff.

Then he went into the outback of Alaska, challenging himself to survive the harsh winter environment by living off the land, ignoring the fact that even the native grizzly bears don't try to eat their way through an Alaskan winter, but curl up in a cave and snore instead.

Unsurprisingly, the young man died. There's a fine line between being courageous and being stupid. My feeling is he'd have been better off "doing" Vipassana, at least until springtime came around — and in a way it takes more courage than wandering around in the Alaskan outback, because you have to look at yourself 24/7.

When you have too much energy, you can't sit down and watch. And when you become a watcher, oftentimes you don't have enough energy. The recipe in this book is how to have both, how to have energy and be a witness. This why Osho talked so much about Zorba the Buddha, because you need to celebrate your energy and you also need to meditate, you need to be able to dance wildly and also sit silently with your eyes closed.

The beauty of working with young people is that I get to suggest to them to develop the knack of finding that inner space of watching, whenever they can remember to do so. Then, when they're older and don't have quite as much energy, they can slip more easily into a regular habit of meditation.

So, I encourage young people to dance, make love, take drugs, go backpacking around the world…do whatever appeals, because when they get older, those same things will take much more effort, maybe requiring more energy than they want to give. But if they have learned the knack of meditation, they will look inside and find a joyful buddha sitting, waiting there, ready to welcome them to another whole dimension of being.

It's like the Buddha is smiling at them and saying, "Hey, did you have a good time out there? Great! Now let's introduce you to your aloneness."

Chapter Twelve

INNER EMPTINESS

Greed is an effort to stuff yourself with something —it may be sex, it may be food, it may be money, it may be power. Greed is the fear of inner emptiness. One is afraid of being empty, and one wants somehow to possess more and more things. One wants to go on stuffing things inside so one can forget one's emptiness. But to forget one's emptiness is to forget one's real self. To forget one's emptiness is to forget the way to god. To forget one's emptiness is the most stupid act in the world that a man is capable of. Osho

Nothing bothers me more than when I go to Thailand and watch parents giving one of their sons to the local temple. The little guy is supposed to be meditating and he looks very cute, as he sits on the floor of the temple with his shaved head, wearing his new orange robe and closing his eyes.

But then, being a kid, he pretty soon dozes off, slumps slowly to one side and eventually falls over. He doesn't get hurt because he's close to the ground and in any case his young bones are soft and supple – no risk of fractures at that age.

This initiation into monkhood would have been a great moment if it had arisen out of a spontaneous feeling within the child. Not that any child would wake up one morning and say, "Mommy, take me to the temple, I've decided to be a Buddhist monk for the rest of my life." If that happened, the guy would probably be enlightened already.

It's not a bad life for a monk in Thailand and some of them do very well for themselves financially, sexually and socially — all behind the curtain of religion, of course, until a scandal leaks out into the media: an all-too-regular occurrence.

What bothers me, as you will probably have guessed, is the lack of respect for individual freedom. The destiny of the child has already been decided by the parents. And, of course, it doesn't happen only in Thailand — that's just an obvious example of something that's universal. To a greater or lesser degree, this is what happens to all of us, at least, until we start to wake up and begin to figure out what's been done to us.

As Osho once said, "The greatest slavery is that of the child."

Your parents didn't give you to a temple, they gave you a template, which is far more subtle. I had no idea what a template was until I became computer literate: it's a pre-formatted document, with a program created by the user. That's what your parents programmed into your mind, setting you out on the road to adulthood with a template that was compatible with society's beliefs and attitudes. So, please wait for that moment that will arrive, sooner or later, depending how quickly you start to wake up, and you ask yourself, *Is this me or is this my parents?*

People have been sitting on you since your very first day out of the womb. In fact, many people get sat on while they are still in the womb, when the parents, with the best of intentions, begin to map out the destiny of the unborn child.

I can tell you how far it can go, because a few years back there was a case in America where a multi-millionaire stock analyst called Jake Grubman was investigated for allegedly giving a more favorable stock valuation to the AT&T telecom giant in exchange for his twin toddlers being accepted at an exclusive preschool in Manhattan.

The investigation gave a rare insight into the intense elitism among wealthy New Yorkers who compete ferociously for limited spaces in a few "hot schools." To be clear, we're not even talking about regular school here, but preschool, or nursery school as it is sometimes called. Just imagine, you're three years old and your parents are already fighting tooth and nail to get you a seat on the American gravy train.

"Getting into the right nursery school will help you get into the right private school which will take you to the right Ivy League college," said a professional New York school placement consultant. She said she'd seen wealthy chief executives of major corporations "reduced to tears" because they were unable to get their kids into the most fashionable nursery schools.

By the way, Grubman was banned for life from the financial industry by the US Securities and Exchange Commission, and fined $15 million, but afterwards he still had $100 million in spare change and continued to do well for himself as managing partner in a high- tech consulting firm.

The sobering reality about this story is that Grubman would have gotten away with his AT&T rating scam, which potentially cost his clients millions of dollars in poor investments, if he hadn't grown over-confident and started boasting to others about his insider accomplishments.

Here's my philosophical take on this sorry tale: one of the basic things we just don't realize, when we look enviously at people with millions, is how little peace of mind wealth really brings. I mean to say: chances are you sometimes catch yourself daydreaming and thinking, *If only I had a million bucks, or maybe a hundred million, all my problems would be solved!*

It ain't necessarily so. Ask our friend Mr. Grubman. Here's a guy with greenbacks spilling out of his pockets and he's so desperate to get his kids into a tiny, snobby, cliquey preschool in uptown Manhattan that he's willing to become a Wall Street crook to clinch the deal.

I mean, Jake Grubman could have hired a dozen tutors that would turn his kids into geniuses without even glancing at the NYC nursery lists. But no. As soon as you reach that dreamed-of elitist financial status and find yourself awash with dollars, a whole new paradigm of comparison and competition opens up to make your even more stressed than you were when making your pile.

With college, it's the same. People spend hundreds of thousands of dollars to get their children into "the right college" and sometimes resort to the weirdest subterfuges to make it happen. A case I remember involved a well-known couple, fashion designer Mossimo Giannulli and actress Lori Loughlin, who paid half a million dollars in bribes to get their two daughters admitted to the University of Southern California (USC) even though their grades weren't high enough for them to qualify.

They used a so-called "mastermind" who'd developed a scam of gaining access for students at various colleges, by bribing sports coaches and administrators to accept them as potential athletes for college sports teams.

The children of Loughlin and Giannulli were admitted to USC on the understanding they would be part of the rowing team, when in reality they'd never seen a scull in their lives and probably couldn't spell it either.

They were accepted at USC but the ruse was exposed when it became obvious these young "athletes" couldn't row across a small pond and back. A number of coaches, administrators and parents went to jail because of the scam and Lori Loughlin herself served two months in prison. Her daughters had to leave the college.

"I thought I was acting out of love for my children, but in reality it only undermined and diminished my daughters' abilities and accomplishments," a remorseful Loughlin said after being busted.

These stories are so crazy that we can all learn from them. For example, these parents had big hearts and big dreams for their kids and wanted the best for them. But what they actually did, as Loughlin acknowledged, was to create embarrassment for the children and lots of trouble for themselves.

And, if we look a little deeper, behind the details of what happened, you can sense the expectations these parents had and the pressure this put on their children. It's the same everywhere.

In New York and Los Angeles, of course, you get the most extreme examples, because the world's most glamorous cities also play host to the world's biggest assholes.

Generally, with the best of intentions, all parents project their dreams and desires on their children, carving a pathway of achievement that runs from nursery school all the way to college graduation, and then onward into top jobs and high-society marriages. It goes on and on, because, for the desiring mind, it's never enough.

There's a neat little epilogue to the Grubman story: after all the best New York private schools had turned their backs on the disgraced financier, he was seen touring a regular public school on Madison Avenue, close to his home, considering it as a possible next step for his twins.

"It's an excellent public school, probably the highest-regarded in the city," commented one educational insider. I don't recall how it turned out in the end, but if Grubman did place his kids there, he saved a small fortune in private school fees. So, perhaps he made a shrewd deal in the end, after all.

Parents love their kids — that's a no-brainer. But parents also damage their kids in the name of love. Parents have big hearts for their children, but those hearts are filled with conditions. They might think their love is unconditional, but wait until those kids morph into rebellious, ungrateful teenagers and then see what happens.

I may be wrong, but I don't think a businessman like Jake Grubman has any idea what bringing up kids involves, especially when it's time to let them fly the coop and find their own way in life. I can almost hear the former telecom consultant complaining to his children, "What about all those years and dollars I invested in you?" as they take off in unplanned directions.

Here's the thing: bringing up kids is not a business. You really don't know who they are, or where they're headed, so the only return on the energy and money you invest in them is to enjoy them here and now, while they are growing up with you.

In business terminology, either you get an immediate return on your investment by accepting them and appreciating them as they are, while they are with you, or you lose out. You can't trade in futures with your kids because you don't know where they're going. As far as getting your reward is concerned, it's literally now or never.

On the subject of hearts, Osho has said some mysterious things in his time and one of them was the way he referred to "the wisdom of the empty heart." This seems odd, I'm sure you'll agree, because normally we are accustomed to think of the heart in terms of being filled with love. We think of a loving heart, a generous heart, a compassionate heart.

Or, on the negative side, we know the heart as a source of passion, such as the pain of heartbreak, the longing of unrequited love, the place where love can turn into hate, and so on. In other words, we think of the heart as being full, not empty.

So what did Osho mean?

By way of answering, let me draw your attention to a word that's not going to win a popularity contest among New Age gurus but could get a few Zen monks nodding their approval. What is that word? Emptiness.

These are two things that are beautiful about meditation: an empty mind, an empty heart. But in the West, the word "emptiness" when used in connection with spirituality seems scary for many people because they think that emptiness has no energy and no meaning. What's more, there's nothing you can "do" with emptiness and, psychologically speaking, in the self-help biz, it's always reassuring to think there's something you can "do" to improve yourself.

So, emptiness looks scary, but in reality it's the key to the door of knowing yourself. In meditation, what we find is that emptiness has its own mysterious qualities. For example:

Emptiness is vibrating – just don't ask with what.

Emptiness has its own fullness – just don't try and give it a name.

Emptiness has its own abundance – but there's no label to put on it.

It doesn't make sense, I know, but this is one of those paradoxical things you have to experience in order to find out it's true. The empty heart only seems empty because we're not accustomed to hanging out there. When we do, we find there is no better space from which to watch the madness of the world than from one's own empty heart.

Maybe I should explain that when Osho, Gautam Buddha, and the Zen mystics refer to the empty heart, they are in reality pointing to the very center of one's own being. From this perspective, all thinking and all emotions, positive and negative, come within the sphere of the mind. The heart, on the other hand, is that which is silent, empty and watching.

"The empty heart is your purity, your virginity. This empty heart opens the door to the universal and the eternal," said my favorite teacher, when I was sitting in discourse with him one fine morning.

So, rather than trying to drop all those difficult emotions that haunt us, like anger and jealousy for example, the easier route is to practice meditation methods as a way of getting in touch with your empty heart. From that inner space, those all-powerful emotions that threaten to sweep us away to disaster have less grip.

By the way, please don't misunderstand me – chances are you will anyway, but that's something else – I'm not against people enjoying a heart bursting with emotion. That's part of being human. For example, you can watch *Titanic* for the umpteenth time and still get overwhelmed and teary-eyed with feelings of romantic tragedy as Leonardo di Caprio sinks beneath the cold Atlantic waves, leaving Kate Winslet alone on her raft.

Enjoy the passion. Have a good cry. You'll have to overlook the fact that Kate seemed way too business-like when she pulled Leo's hands off the edge of her raft and let him sink. Okay, he was already dead, but still, it almost looked like she was smiling when she did it. And as movie director James Cameron has already been told many times – it really irritates him, so let's say it again – that raft looked big enough for two, so how come Leo didn't climb aboard and live with Kate happily ever after?

You know what Cameron said, when bugged by a journalist on this point for the umpteenth time? He flushed red in the face and snapped, "Wait a minute, let's call Will Shakespeare and ask him why Romeo and Juliet had to die!"

Anyway, getting back on track, what I'm saying is: just because the empty heart is your ultimate reality, that doesn't mean you cannot enjoy, and also suffer, the whole spectrum of human emotions. After all, if we weren't meant to have emotions, they wouldn't be there in the first place, right?

As you may have noticed, this book is about being alive in a new, fresh, and multi- dimensional way. So, what I am suggesting is an exploration of your own inner emptiness, because you will discover that the more empty you become through meditation, the more energy you have and the more alive you feel.

Your parents had great intentions, it's just that they were not enlightened enough to do it right because they were worried about you rather than checking in with themselves. And like I said earlier, as part of their concern, instead of giving you space and love, they filled you with the rules and regulations of how to fit in with society, plus all the extra information society would like you to have.

In meditation, when you get a taste of No Mind, you start to see that mind is a hodge- podge of all your thoughts and all your conditioning. It's a madhouse in there. It's a circus. One thought leads to another thought and that thought leads you somewhere else and before you know it you're somewhere in outer space making love with a female alien and thinking you're both being sucked by gravity into a black hole and are probably both doomed unless Einstein's theory of spacetime can rescue you....

Okay, I'm kidding. But you know this about your mind, right? You know how out of control it can be and how it leads you all over the place.

A friend of mine once asked Osho a question in which he expressed his worry about too much thinking and pleaded, "Help! My mind is going bananas!"

I loved Osho's reply. He said, "Mind cannot go bananas. Mind *is* bananas!"

Ain't that the truth. So, this book is really a guide to help you get in touch with your innocence again, the innocence you had before your parents gave you the template, before all the information about society came pouring into you.

It's about remembering that point in your life when you didn't know anything at all. You didn't know what you liked. You didn't know what you hated. You just were saying "Thank you, I am alive and everything is wonderful."

But of course it didn't last. We lost our innocence even before we realized we had it and we grew up into these monsters called "citizens of the world." Nobody asked the world if it wanted us as its citizens but here we are, more and more of us each day, all trying to climb aboard the gravy train, all wanting a bit more elbow room, a bit more money, a bit more privilege.

As a citizen of the world, I'm inviting you to come more from silence and less from the noise of the mind. Because unless you are meditating, all you will find in your mind is one big traffic jam. Or maybe not exactly a gridlock, because your mind is always moving, so let's say it's more like a slow, crowded, freeway crawl in LA at four o'clock on a Friday afternoon, when everyone's trying to get the fuck out of town for the weekend, and you're praying the angry-looking guy who just cut in ahead of you doesn't get a fit of road rage, pull out a gun, and start venting his emotions via a drive-by shooting spree.

My feeling is, when you get to the point where you are not so identified with your thoughts, then you are not so identified with yourself as a person — the person you always thought you were — and then you can have a better life.

But that is my feeling. You may read this book as a comedy of errors, thinking *How crazy is this guy, he is so entertaining!* Well, I'm happy you find me entertaining because that's the way I like to share myself. But don't think for a second that I'm not also laughing at you.

Why am I laughing? Because I think you are crazy for not being yourself.

Chapter Thirteen

WITNESSING IS YOUR SECRET LOVE

Be silent, close your eyes. Feel your body to be completely frozen. Look inwards, as deep as possible. It is your own space. At the very end you will find the empty heart.

The empty heart is a door to eternity. It is a connection between you and existence. It is not something physical or material. It is not something mental or psychological. It is something beyond both, transcending both. It is your spirituality. Remember, the empty heart makes you a buddha.

This moment is blessed. Ten thousand hearts are feeling the silence and the merger with existence. You are the fortunate ones of the earth.

Relax... just be a watcher of mind and body both. The insistence should be on the witnessing.

Witnessing is your secret love. Witnessing is Buddha, watching. Osho

This book is not about quitting life, it is about watching life, so that you can begin to put your energy in directions that fulfill you, that make you excited to get up in the morning, instead of wanting to sleep in.

Of course, when you are tired you can rightfully enjoy a couple of extra hours of sleep in the morning, but so many people want to sleep in because they just don't want to get up. Many people who do get up, decide to have a cup of coffee rather than spending a few minutes meditating and watching their breath. But when people are excited to get up, enjoy a cup of coffee, then spend some time meditating and watching their breath, that for me is the optimum way to start the day.

This book is for those of you who have been living your lives without energy, not only sleeping in bed but also sleeping even when you are walking around pretending to be awake. The idea of the book is you need to get out of your spiritual bed, shake off the slumber, wipe the sleep dust out of your eyes, realize you're living in a prison and plan your escape.

What prison? Well, for example, the prison you call "home." Because unless you are awake and free, your home is a prison. Once you are free, your home is just a home, somewhere you can relax and rest.

Speaking of prisons, here's a little fantasy: let's pretend you are a woman who just met a great guy. You flirt with him, you touch his arm, you kind of let him know that you would like to play. And, because you don't trust yourself, as soon as you get that guy home, you turn your home into a prison for him, too. You lock the front door, close the windows and make the house so secure that he can't leave.

Or, just to embrace some gender equality, let's pretend you are a guy who just met a wonderful woman. You flirt with her, impress her with your knowledge, your car, your job, your credit cards…guys, you know how it goes. And, because you don't trust yourself, you also cannot trust this beautiful woman, so, as soon as you bring her home and succeed in closing the bedroom door, you start worrying about how to "make her mine."

You want to possess her, maybe for keeps — at least, that's what it seems like in the first flush of a new attraction. You want her as a trophy, like that stuffed tiger's head on the wall that your grandfather shot in India. And when it comes to the next cocktail party or fancy social gathering, you want her to be hanging adoringly on your arm when you make your entrance, not the arm of some other creep.

What are we looking at here? Well, for sure, we're noticing how insecure we are, we're seeing how possessive we need to be in order to feel safe, how desperate we are to avoid the pain of loneliness, or heartbreak, or humiliation, or jealousy, or any of those horrible feelings that can rise up and swamp us when relationships come unglued. We've taken a look at some of that already.

There are lots of ways of looking at ourselves when it comes to making our way through the labyrinth of life, and I want to focus attention for a moment on the issue of image — how we like to present ourselves to the world and how we want to be seen in the eyes of others.

Of course, concern over image has been going on since civilization began — if it ever did — and certainly since the time of Genesis when Jacob commented, "My brother Esau is a hairy man, but I am a smooth man." I guess hairy and smooth have been competing with each other, going in and out of fashion, ever since. I'm on the hairy side myself, but I haven't experienced it as a drawback, so far.

Image has always been part of human social life, but I don't think image has ever been such a massive issue as it is today. It's simply huge. It's taken over our lives, thanks to the creation of the internet, the worldwide web, social networks, mobile phones, mobile phone cameras, and mobile phone apps.

For example, in terms of self-image, did you ever think you'd see a video clip of Krishna Prem making love with Natalie Portman? Or with Emma Watson? Or Scarlett Johansson? That's the ultimate, right? The camera doesn't lie. That's the living proof that I'm king of the hill, the alpha male of the pack.

Well, I'll be the first to admit that the odds of it happening in real life are about a zillion to one. But it can easily happen as a deepfake video. Now please, you computer nerds out there, don't take this as a challenge to create what I'm saying! I'm a respectable old man and I have a reputation to protect…er, well, maybe not such a great reputation, but there's no need to make it worse.

Deepfakes intrigue me because they serve as a mirror, both to the society around us and to ourselves. I mean, for example, what about these images we put out on Facebook, Instagram and other social media platforms? Are they real? Are they an authentic reflection of who we really are, or are they our own version of deepfake?

We'll talk more about that in a moment, but first let's take a look at an area of computer technology that's not just blowing people's minds but imitating their faces to a scary degree.

Deepfake apps are already on the market, waiting for you to download, and then you can do practically anything you want with your favorite movie stars, rock musicians, singers and politicians.

I guess I'm a little slow. I thought this deepfake stuff was in its infancy and only reclusive techies knew how to use this software. Not one bit. It's here, anyone can download it, and believe me, people are downloading these apps, big time.

According to one report I read, a deepfake app that was newly launched on the market was downloaded 100,000 times in its first month. This gives you the power to create your own deepfakes, but if you're lazy and want to get your rocks off by watching famous people in sexual action you don't even have to do that.

You can go to deepfake porn websites, type in the name of your favorite actress, and watch her doing all kinds of…well…porn. Her face has been superimposed on a female model and she's banging away. Apparently, it's all perfectly legal.

In the old days, meaning, back in 1995, there was a big hoo-hah when a private videotape was stolen from the house of *Baywatch* star Pamela Anderson and her boyfriend Tommy Lee. It showed Pamela and Tommy making love and it went viral.

A few years later, a similar tape showing Paris Hilton making love also became a massive hit with the public. And a third sex tape, this one of Kim Kardashian making love with rapper Ray J, was "leaked" in 2007 – either deliberately or accidentally – and paved the path to stardom for the reality TV actress.

But these days, in our brave, new, digitally enhanced world, you don't need to wait for a real-life sex scandal to burst out of a celebrity's bedroom. You can make your own videos, with your own favorite stars.

There is a darker, nastier side to this new technology. It's called "revenge porn." In the past, this has meant that two silly teenagers, or young adults, in the first hot flush of a love affair, decide to make an intimate video of themselves. Later, they break up, one of them feels hurt, then posts the video to humiliate and embarrass his or her former partner.

But now you don't need to wait for the love affair to happen. If you can manage to pull together a few photos of your local victim, you can deepfake a porn video without even shaking hands or saying hello, let alone going to bed.

As a side issue, I want to draw your attention, once again, to my favorite mass entertainment company, Disney, and how its efforts to sugarcoat reality sometimes get spectacularly derailed.

For example, one of their recent teenage icons was Bella Thorne, who began her career as a goody-goody child star in the kind of wholesome teenage soaps that Walt Disney and his merry men have made famous.

But then, as soon as she became an adult, Thorne broke out of the stereotype, first by declaring she was bisexual, then pansexual — a new category, meaning attraction to all genders, or regardless of genders — and then she went on to direct an adult film called *Her & Him* in conjunction with Pornhub.

I have to chuckle at Disney. This is the second time they've created a too-good-to-be- true female teenage star who cut loose when she became an adult. The other, of course, was Miley Cyrus, who was a Disney teen idol in the hit series *Hannah Montana*. Next thing Disney knew, this wholesome young lady was swinging naked on a wrecking ball.

Anyway, what I wanted to say was that some criminal creeps stole topless photos of Bella Thorne and then tried to blackmail her, threatening to splash them all over the media if she didn't pay up. What she did was great: she pre-empted the creeps by publishing the photos herself. That takes guts!

Bella Thorne has also written a tell-all book about her own life, including years of being sexually abused as a child and bouts of depression and drug taking. It's titled *The Life of a Wannabe Mogul* and no, I haven't read it, because I only just heard about this young woman, but I did read a reviewer's comment that explains why she impresses me:

"You can tell she wrote it for herself and nothing else: not for fame, money, legacy, to impress someone or to prove something. It's her way of revealing the real Bella Thorne to the world, regardless of their opinions."

Now, here is someone who doesn't give a damn about her image. Or, maybe I should say, she trusts in herself to such an extent that she is prepared to show people her true self- image, as she really is. In an age when we're seeing multiple layers of social fakeness, that's an awesome achievement for a 23-year-old.

Incidentally, Bella Thorne has the dubious privilege of being portrayed in the most deepfake porn videos, and she has predicted the abuse won't stop with public figures. "You can do it to your best friend at school," she warned.

She went on to ask this very pertinent question to the designers and creators of deepfake software: "Why would you even put this thing out there when you know what a huge percentage of the world is going to do with that?"

The answer, of course, is mainly to do with money, although I guess there are some techies who just want to create the perfect deepfake software because it's a challenge waiting to be mastered. Like Everest, if it's there, waiting to be conquered, someone's gonna want to be the first to the summit.

Now, let's take a long, deep breath and swim our way up to the surface, from going deeply down into the muddy waters of fake videos. Let's look at the behavior of us ordinary citizens and see how our images are reflected on Facebook, Instagram, and other social networks.

What's it all about? Or maybe I should ask the same question in a more direct and personal way: "How deepfake are you? Is your social profile really you?"

In a nutshell, social media invites us to create the image of ourselves we want the world to see. We carefully sanitize ourselves to look our best. And then, for sure, we want to be liked for what we present, and we watch carefully to see how many likes we get, compared to our friends.

For old geezers like me, it's not so important. I mean, it's nice to get lots of likes on a photo I post, or for an article I write, but I've spent a good deal of time cleaning up my psychological basement, not to mention my attic, so my issues of self-worth and self-esteem tend not to be so fragile. I'm not gonna jump off the Golden Gate Bridge if I get fewer than 200 likes, right?

For young people, it can be more serious. In those tender years when we are still figuring out who we are and whether we're accepted by our peers, it can be a very big deal if you lag far behind the most popular kids on the social network. Comparisons like these will shape your psychology, creating a positive or negative image of yourself, depending on how successful you are at making friends and gathering a following.

This is a computerized extension of what we've been doing all along. In my youth, it was the same: some kids were popular in high school and did well socially, while others, for a number of reasons, faltered in their friendships and retreated into the shadows.

When you think about it, life is a strange business. First, we need to develop an ego that works for us in the world, that wins us friends, dates and a career, then we meet a guy like Osho and suddenly discover that we need to drop that ego again.

It's even stranger when you think that we haven't been educated or trained for any of this. We learn the three Rs at school, but we don't have lessons in how to deal with the challenges of peer pressure, the compelling need to conform, social rejection and acceptance, self-esteem and all this personal stuff, which can make school heaven or hell, depending on whether you get the lucky breaks or end up being bullied and crying in a corner.

Anyway, the good news is, you made it this far. You must be okay, to some degree, otherwise you wouldn't be reading this book. So congratulations on making it through your childhood and your teens, and welcome to this introduction to your essential aloneness.

Here's the bottom line: no matter what happens to you socially, whether you become a teen idol, a porn star, a social reject, a rock musician, a good-time guru with his own channel on YouTube...whatever hand Fate decides to deal to you, it all comes down to one thing in the end: you are alone.

If we can anchor ourselves in this ultimate reality, then we can easily ride the tide of the ever-moving social river. We can make friends, we can fall in love, we can become famous or just carry on being a regular guy or gal, knowing that it all comes and goes, rises and falls like the Dow Jones Index, and beneath it all we are, as we have always been, alone.

It feels weird, doesn't it? It seems hard to embrace the simple, self-evident truth of our aloneness when boyfriends and girlfriends, husbands and wives, children and parents, friends and enemies, are all so important to us. They mean so much to us. How can these powerful bonds be so unreal?

Well, as a matter of fact, I don't go along with the Hindu philosophy that the world is an illusion. To me, the world is real. There's only one thing to remember: it is impermanent. Nothing lasts. As George Harrison once wisely said: "All things must pass." Or, to quote Gautam Buddha, "That which is subject to origination is also subject to cessation."

Samsara, the great wheel of life and death, turns endlessly, and we must somehow understand that the essential core of our being is free from its grip, even if the rest of our psyche feels chained to the spokes.

When did Mark Zuckerberg invent Facebook? I guess it was just after the turn of the millennium. Originally intended for students at Harvard, it now has 2.7 billion monthly users worldwide. In its wake came Instagram, TikTok, Snapchat, Pinterest, Twitter…I'm sure there are others I haven't even heard about yet.

But the thing is, Facebook and the other networks aren't new. We've done this stuff before. No matter how old we are, or when we were born, we've always been using some kind of Facebook app — not literally, but in a manner of speaking. We've always had a face that we want to show the world, even before computers were invented. Why? Because that's the name of the ego game. We want to look good in front of other people.

How do we go beyond the ego? Let's look at it in terms of the Christian cross, not as a declaration of faith in JC, but as a spiritual symbol: two intersecting lines depicting the two possibilities of human experience.

The horizontal line represents three-dimensional spacetime, moving from the past through the present into the future. We are born, we grow up, we get into all kinds of trouble, we grow old and die. Meanwhile, millions of other people are doing the same.

Then there is the vertical line, which has nothing to do with time. It has to do with going deeper and deeper into this present moment, here and now.

Right this moment, reading this book, you are moving through horizontal time. Then you put the book down, close your eyes and meditate. If you bring yourself totally to this moment, you are no longer moving from Point A thru Point B to Point C.

Yes, that process will continue outside of you, but inside you will find that another process is beginning. You are moving vertically from Point A to a deeper experience of A, then moving to an even deeper experience of A…and so on.

By the way, as you may have noticed, when you move vertically like this, there's nobody else around. You are moving deeper and deeper into yourself, and the only person you are going to meet there is you. This, my friend, is your aloneness.

You may also notice that in this present moment, there is no room for thinking, because mind cannot operate in this kind of vertical space. And because there are no thoughts, there is also no sense of "I" because "I" is also a kind of thought.

As a consequence, you still know you exist, as pure consciousness, but you know there is no you. Welcome to the ultimate paradox: you are, but at the same time you are not. Your ego has vanished.

So, sit down in your living room and take it easy. Have a cup of tea.

Chapter Fourteen

SOUND AND SILENCE

When for the first time you fall in love, you meet the opposite. Immediately, it is as if you have got wings, you can fly; poetry arises in your heart. What is happening? The opposite has created something in you. Silence alone is not very beautiful, sound alone is not very beautiful, but the meeting of sound and silence is very, very beautiful -- that is music. The meeting of silence and sound is music. Osho

In Pune, I had two good friends, Deva Premal & Miten. You may know them personally, or, most probably, you know them because they broke out into the New Age mainstream in the late nineties with a stunningly beautiful recording of the *Gayatri Mantra*, which is an ancient Sanskrit chant that in Hindu religious culture is said to date back about 5,000 years.

In fact, that album featuring the Gayatri Mantra, which is titled *The Essence*, became the definitive sound for anyone who ever went to a yoga class. Okay, I'm exaggerating a little here, but honestly that's how it got to be well known, because at the end of every yoga class, especially in the US, all the participants lie down on their yoga mats and relax in a position called *Savasana*.

Then the yoga teacher plays some soothing spiritual music to round off the class and that's how the amazingly pure sound of Premal's voice became famous. It was recognized by yoga teachers everywhere as the perfect way to end a class. Why? Because Premal didn't just sing the mantra. She *became* the mantra and transmitted its awesome beauty to the world.

Or, maybe I should say she gave it to the whole world except India, because since forever it has been one of the most revered prayers of the Hindu tradition and millions of Indians recite it to themselves several times a day.

When you hear the story behind how the Gayatri Mantra came to Premal, you kinda get shivers down your spine because it was almost like her destiny — as if she was born to deliver it to us all.

Premal says she began her journey with the mantra in her mother's womb, when her father got into the habit of chanting the Gayatri Mantra to her daily. The mantra continued to be her bedtime lullaby sung by her father and her mother after she was born, which occurred around 1970 in Germany.

Many years later, in 1990, she was visiting the Osho Resort in Pune where she was learning meditation and also studying all kinds of bodywork and energy work. There, she met the guy who was destined to become her life partner, an English musician called Miten. They've been together since 1992 and have also been touring since then.

They had humble beginnings. For example, I recall being in a men's group in the Pune resort and one night, as part of our male bonding, we decided to stay up until dawn. First, we did a sweat lodge together and then, at some godforsaken hour in the early morning, we all gathered in a soundproof group room — so as not to incur the wrath of our sleeping friends — and we were joined by Premal and Miten who spent a sweet hour with us singing Osho songs. I don't think it's any secret to admit that, in the beginning, Miten was running the show.

He was an experienced musician and had previously attained "almost famous" status by opening for English bands on tour like The Kinks and Fleetwood Mac. Premal had no experience, but she possessed a naturally beautiful voice, and since the two were anyway becoming lovers it was a no-brainer they would start singing together.

Together, Miten and Premal released a couple of albums that were well received among their sannyasin friends. Then, in 1998, they recorded *The Essence* and that was a game changer for both of them. It's kinda neat to note they made that recording in the house of Premal's mother, so it was a funky start to a great album.

I bumped into them at a time when they were planning to travel once more to Premal's mother to make their next album, but when they told me their plans I shook my head and said, "You can't do that! It was magic the first time, but now you need to be professionals. Now you need to hire a proper producer in a proper recording studio."

They got nervous and Miten said to me, "I don't know if we have enough money to do that."

And I said, "I will give you the money because I am convinced it will sell well. And you can pay me back later from your sales, so don't be worried about it."

Well, as you can guess, their careers were taking off, so they didn't need to borrow money from me, but they remained grateful. The lesson here is that sometimes, when you offer somebody space, they grow into it, and that is another message in this book: instead of looking at how many people sit on you, look instead towards the people who give you space.

Those are the people you want to talk to, because even though they may not be able to write out a check, they will know how to give you space. Out of that space, you can become creative.

Miten and Premal have done well; now they are at the top of their game. Every time they do a concert and I'm in the area, they invite me as their guest to sit in the front row. And these concerts are special because they are full of meditators, so the love that Premal and Miten share with us goes full circle as we love them right back. Meditators know how to share in this way, giving energy back to whoever is sharing a performance with them.

By the way, speaking of performances, I'm sure some of you know that the American singer and actress Cher, also known as "The Goddess of Pop" fell in love with the Gayatri Mantra when she heard Premal's recording at a yoga class.

Cher also wanted to record it and, naturally enough, her recording company asked her who wrote the song. In the dollar-driven world of American showbiz, you even need to ask who wrote an ancient mantra — that's just how it is among corporate executives and their lawyers. She told them it's considered to be the oldest song that was ever written.

Out of her magnificence, Cher invited Premal and Miten to one of her shows and that night announced that the writers of the

Gayatri Mantra were in the audience. So, Premal and Miten stood up and they got a standing ovation. They also got a check with the royalty payment because Premal's version was so beautiful and inspired Cher to follow her. Anyway, the real authors had been dead for 5,000 years and probably their copyright had expired.

Cher included the Gayatri Mantra in her Farewell Tour of 2002-2005 and I have to say, even though I love the woman dearly, I was disappointed when I watched her version on television, because it was overdone. Well, Cher always did have a taste for theatrical costumes and stage sets ranging from elaborate to fantastic to downright-bizarre, so after a bunch of semi-naked guys with Indian turbans had danced around the stage for a while, she came out on a mechanical elephant and sang the Gayatri Mantra, dressed up as some kind of Indian princess.

It was good showbiz and Cher sang it well — of course, because she has a great voice and strong stage presence. But it was a performance, not a transmission. It was entertainment, not spirituality. But then again, there's always been a fine and shifting line between the two, right?

During his life, George Harrison crossed and recrossed that line many times and after his death, on the life-size statue representing him and the rest of the Fab Four, unveiled a few years ago in [Liverpool](), the Gayatri Mantra was shown engraved on his belt, symbolizing a landmark event in his life. I don't know what that landmark event was but, knowing George, it probably had something to do with either LSD or India.

By the way, as some of you are aware, Premal and Miten performed for [the Dalai Lama]() in Munich in 2002 during a conference titled "Unity in Duality," which brought leading figures from the world of science together with members of the global Buddhist community.

Premal and Miten gave a concert at the conference and were also invited to sing for the Dalai Lama at a small pre-conference gathering. They'd heard that the Dalai Lama's favorite mantra was the Tara Mantra, dedicated to the Green Tara of Compassion, and that he had requested his monks to chant it for him when he was ill, so they also sang it for him.

I love the conference title "Unity in Duality." It kind of sums up everything. Apparently, so I'm told, this concept is rooted in an ancient Tibetan teaching which sees all dualities — science and religion, energy and matter, spiritualism and materialism, good and evil — as temporary conditions that rise and fall, with a beginning and an ending, within the context of an overall, universal, unifying force.

Naturally, the Dalai Lama was speaking at the Munich conference and he was the main attraction for the media. This prompts me to reflect on his international public image, in the context of what we were talking about in the previous chapter, because it seems to me that the Dalai Lama is a most interesting character.

For one thing, unlike the vast majority of people, here's a guy who is well aware of his aloneness, by which I mean his inner core of nothingness, or emptiness, and that's why in recent years we've seen a rash of cartoon jokes about him on the social networks.

You know the ones: it's the Dalai Lama's birthday and he's been given a present and he's opening a box, which turns out to be empty. And he's beaming with happiness and saying, "Just what I've always wanted for my birthday... Nothing!"

As for me, I've always wanted a private audience with "His Holiness" to ask him, "Your Holiness, you've spent fourteen lifetimes being the Dalai Lama, but is that really you? Who are you, behind the role? And if you haven't been able to become enlightened in fourteen lifetimes, coming back each time as such a spiritually advanced dude, wouldn't it be better to come back next time as a truck driver?"

It's just a fantasy. I don't think we're destined to meet in this lifetime. Maybe in the next. Anyway, he's a really nice guy and I wouldn't want to upset him. And besides, he has already said that when he becomes 90 years old, he will let us know if he'll be coming back again as the Dalai Lama, or whether he's going to be the last incarnation. Right now, he's 85, so it won't be long now before we learn if the fifteenth is a sure bet or a no-show.

Incidentally, I find it hilarious that the Chinese Government, which is officially atheist, is trying to dictate how and when the Dalai Lama should incarnate next time.

In a statement issued in 2015, the Chinese said, "Whether the Dalai Lama wants to cease reincarnation or not, this decision is not up to him."

Can you believe it? In the first place, they don't believe any of this religious stuff. In the second place, they're going to decide his next life for him. So, even if he says that he's not coming back, or coming back incognito next time, the Chinese will still "find" him and appoint his new incarnation.

We innocent Westerners tend to think that if it wasn't for the nasty Chinese everything would be sweetness and light in Tibet, but when you look into the history of reincarnating lamas and monks you find all kinds of squabbles and quarrels between powerful families and different factions. For example, the post of the Dalai Lama traditionally came with gold, land, and patronage, so naturally it was tempting for powerful people to "discover" the new Dalai Lama as a member of their own family.

Frankly, with so much political infighting down through the centuries, if the present Dalai Lama has really been the same guy in all of those previous thirteen incarnations, without a break, it would indeed be a miracle.

But, like I say, the fourteenth Dalai Lama is a really nice guy who wants to make the world a better place. So, on a practical level, in terms of helping ordinary folks, one of the things the Dalai Lama emphasizes in his teachings is the need to feel grateful for this gift of life.

He's not alone. I'm happy to see that, on a wider spiritual basis involving many different teachings and teachers, a lot of people are getting into this concept of "Thank You."

Personally, I love what the Sufi mystic Rumi said, "If you are going to pray once a day, make that prayer, 'Thank you.'"

Every moment of your life, you have the opportunity to look for a way to say "Thank you." It is beneficial and healthy, maybe it's the most healthy thing we can do for ourselves.

But we're all human, right, so just between you and me, I'm not expecting you to be able to say "Thank you" when somebody just stole your car, or your girlfriend, or your new iPhone. Let's be generous in such unpleasant moments and allow ourselves a few minutes, or hours, to be really upset.

Maybe your "thank you" doesn't come for a while, because being grateful doesn't mean that your daily survival needs will be guaranteed from now on. It doesn't mean that bread will come floating down from the sky. It's not going to rain loaves and fishes any time soon — I've always wondered how JC did that trick, but please don't tell me. Some things are better left as mysteries.

And speaking of gratitude, earlier in this book I was recalling my 17-year love affair with a Dutch woman called Jwala. One day I said to her, "I am thinking about becoming celibate and I know you are not ready because I am older than you. So you should go out and have a date."

I didn't mean she should not come back home — that was a big shock. And that's the trouble with magnanimous gestures based on false assumptions. I wasn't looking at the situation from a feminine perspective. I mean to say...well, I don't like to generalize, but men tend to enjoy a date and then want to come back home to a longtime girlfriend. Women tend to go on a date, fall in love and stay there. And that's what happened with Jwala.

Fortunately, I loved Jwala enough to meet her new boyfriend. The beauty of it was, when the two of them first met, Jwala and I were still together, we were still lovers. But then, as the new guy started falling in love with her, my continued participation in the story became a real problem for him.

He said to Jwala, "I can't sleep at night, I am jealous."

Jwala and I laughed because by that stage in our relationship we were making love like old friends, almost like having a cup of tea at the end of the meal; whereas, because he was her new lover, making love was a really big deal for him.

So Jwala said to me, "How should we handle this?" I said, "Do you love this guy?"

She said, "Yeah."

And I said, "Well, I love you but as we both know, drinking tea together isn't such a big deal anymore. I think we should just drop the idea of tea. We don't need tea. Maybe I will switch to coffee because there are other people in the world and I don't want to disturb your new love affair.

"What is more important to me is that I don't want to disturb our friendship. I don't want to lose you as a friend. And I don't want you to lose him as your new beloved. So let's just drop the tea."

There are many kinds of love and it'll come as no surprise to you when I say that one of those kinds is sexual union. Of course, we know nature has a job to do, which is to create children and perpetuate the species, but now that I am a little older nature doesn't seem to need me for that particular purpose.

Or does it? Jwala is getting older, too, and she is going through menopause. By the way, just as a quick aside, I think men go through menopause, too, but it is not so visible and is usually categorized as "a midlife crisis."

Jwala and I enjoy a laugh about it, because even though Jwala is younger than me she can no longer have a baby — not that she ever wanted one in the first place — but Krishna Prem can still make one. I often wondered why nature would do that.

My feeling is it has something to do with the foolishness of nations and religions, and whatever happened before nations and religions got started — tribes, I guess they were called. Periodically, two different nations, or religions, or tribes, would get angry and start beating the crap out of each other, and then all the young men on both sides would rush off to war and get killed.

So, just in case none of them come back — I mean, usually some of them do, so it's a theoretical situation — then nature has kept the old men in reserve, so they can help all those single young women and young widows to have babies, thereby fulfilling nature's evolutionary demand to perpetuate the species.

Now, I have never heard of this before, so I don't know if it is true. But it does create fantasies which I really shouldn't tell you about, of Krishna Prem having to make love to every young woman who happens to read this book after the Third World War has happened.

Can you imagine? I could be wrong. So, be sure to look out the window. If there is no war going on out there, don't write to me, but if the world is erupting in a massive conflict, please give me a call.

Okay, this is getting a little off track, but then it's my story, so, as far as I'm concerned, it can go where it likes. This book has a life of its own and the story tells itself.

Besides, as you know perfectly well, you can never get enlightened reading somebody else's story. You can only get enlightened by looking at your own life with new eyes. Here I am sharing myself, telling you some of the things I've learned along the way, but what I am hoping is that you will finish reading this book, close it, smile and say:

"Krishna, I am willing to look at my life."

That's it. And that's enough.

Chapter Fifteen

WATCH YOUR THOUGHTS

This is the time for everybody to meditate. This is the time that, except for meditation, nothing can help you to get out of your misery. And meditation is a simple phenomenon. Just whenever you have time, sit silently, doing nothing. Relax, close your eyes, watch your thoughts as if you are watching a movie on the screen. You are just a watcher. If you can watch your thoughts just as if they are moving there on the screen, and you are not involved in them, they start dispersing. It is your involvement that gives them life energy. When you withdraw yourself and become just a witness, thoughts start falling, like leaves which are dead start falling from the trees. Soon you will be surprised, the screen is empty.

Consciousness coming back to the original source is what I call enlightenment. This blissfulness is something that happens here and now.
Osho

We all watch the television news, right? Even those of us who don't make a habit of it tune in sometimes. For example, when the twin towers of the World Trade Center came crashing down, or when Princess Diana's funeral took place in London, or

President Donald Trump lost his re-election bid in November 2020.

It all unfolded in front of our eyes as we switched channels to CNN or one of the big news networks. We were part of it. We were participants. We were there. We felt it, as it happened. Our minds and our feelings were engaged in the drama.

Sometimes it's hard to remember that what we're seeing is not happening to us. Why? Because we get so identified. This can happen with anything. For example, we start watching a football game and, even though we're not fanatic supporters of either team, we pretty soon get identified with one team or the other, hoping for victory and fearing defeat.

But these events are not happening to us. They are happening in front of us, or, maybe I should say they are happening somewhere else on the planet, and are being reproduced on a TV screen in front of our eyes, in our living room.

Watching TV, we acknowledge that we are part of an entirely new human species that can see everything happening around the world without stepping even a foot outside our homes. And what we see affects us, touches us, triggers our feelings and opinions.

However, there's another opportunity opening up for us here: we can watch ourselves watching. That's the only way to become dis-identified with what we're seeing. Ordinary watching won't do, because pretty soon we'll find ourselves caught up in the drama.

In fact, that's what CNN and other news networks are hoping. They want to hook us and pull us in. They want to catch our attention and keep it, because that's how they keep their ratings high and out-compete other television networks.

Psychologically, it's well known by now that negative news stories catch and keep our attention more powerfully than positive news. So, naturally, no news channel is going to open its evening slot with the announcement "Everything's pretty much okay in the USA this evening."

That's a recipe for disaster. I recall reading about one TV news station that decided to show only positive news for 24 hours. Its viewing figures dropped by two thirds.

Viewers instinctively switch to news channels where something really dramatic is happening. And if the networks don't deliver, this has serious financial consequences. When you lose your viewers, your ratings start sinking, the advertising drops off, the quarterly returns go sliding downwards and the guy holding down the job of Chief News Editor is looking for a new career.

How many of you remember Ted Koppel, the journalist who anchored ABC's long- running *Nightline News* for 25 years? For millions of people, Ted Koppel *was* the news. He never had to look for another job. Yet, to me, every evening, the guy looked like an absolute dickhead because every few minutes he'd have to announce a commercial break saying, "We'll be back after these messages...."

So, there you are, sitting in your living room, and you've just been watching some really intense news report about a mass shooting at a school in Texas when, boom, you're being urged to eat sugar-frosted cornflakes for breakfast, or snack on a high-calorie candy bar, or use some fancy-smelling shampoo on your hair....

And then, boom, you're back with Koppel, who's managing somehow to string it all together and look like he's doing a crucial job, whereas in reality he's part-time news anchor, part-time salesman for Kellogg's, Snickers, Pantene, L'Oreal, or Head & Shoulders.

I remember when Koppel interviewed Osho, back in 1985, when he was behind bars in Charlotte, North Carolina. He'd been arrested without a warrant, getting off a plane, and was rumored to be trying to leave the country.

I couldn't believe Koppel. He spent most of the interview trying to trick Osho over his use of the words "friends" and "disciples," and then bitching about Osho's 93 Rolls-Royces. I found myself thinking, *Okay, Ted, make Osho look like a charlatan if you must, but that's not why the guy is in jail!*

Maybe Koppel didn't like Osho. That was okay by me, because Osho was never going to win a popularity contest in the USA, or anywhere else. In disliking him, Koppel was joining a long line of people who stretched half-way around the planet.

But, as far as I was aware, you can't be put in jail for being disliked and there's nothing illegal about stuffing your garage with expensive cars, or saying you don't have disciples, just friends.

So, after grilling Osho, I was expecting Koppel to give the federal law enforcers an equally hard time for keeping him in jail without explaining why they'd arrested him in the first place. Did Koppel do it? No, he did not. What did he say instead?

Yes, you guessed it: "We'll be back after these messages...."

But, as usual, I've gone off track. What I'd like to say is that if you watch CNN, or any news channel, as an ordinary citizen of the world, it is going to mess up your mind. You don't need an army of media researchers to tell you that the more you watch images of suffering, chaos and death on TV, the more your personal stress and anxiety levels are going to rise and the more pessimistic your world view is likely to be.

This book is about watching CNN in a meditative frame of mind, from the back row of the movie house, so to speak. Yes, I know, you're in your living room, not a cinema, but I'm saying "as if" CNN is a movie and you are sitting in the back row of the movie house, munching popcorn and sipping soda.

Why the back row? Well, this gives you distance from the news and also gives you the opportunity to watch that you're watching. It's an invitation to you from me to learn the knack of awareness, like adding a sixth sense, or, as they say in India, opening your third eye.

It goes like this: you're aware that some cool-looking, clean shaven young man in a sharp-looking suit is talking about an earthquake that just happened in Chile, destroying buildings and killing hundreds of people, and at the same time you're aware that you're aware.

This awareness is not a thought. If it was a thought, you'd be caught in what they call "an infinite regress" in which you'd be aware that you're aware that you're aware... and so on. Nope. This is no mind game, my friend, so we don't need to join John Lennon in "playing those mind games forever."

This is for real. This is consciousness at work. Whatever we are watching, we can be aware that we are watching.

And that reminds me…okay, I'll come back to the subject of watching the news in a moment, because I have just remembered Osho's remarks about the movies — the real movies, I mean, in the cinemas.

You know, of course, that I'm American, that's my culture, so of course I've been watching movies all my life. So, I just had to sit up and take notice when Osho started recalling his childhood days, when his father took him to the local movie house in the city of Jabalpur, in Central India.

Osho said he was puzzled, because he was looking around the cinema and seeing people weeping, with tears streaming down their faces. When he mentioned it to his father, he was told "Of course, with such a tragic scene, the whole hall was crying!"

Osho objected, "But nothing is happening. There is only a screen and nothing else.

Nobody is killed, just pictures moving on a screen."

Now here's the thing: Osho said to his father that he could enjoy the film, but he was completely disidentified with the characters and didn't see any enjoyment in crying.

"I can see it as a film," he said. "But I don't want to become part of it."

Now for me, raised on a diet of undiluted Hollywood, most of the enjoyment of going to the movies is to get lost in the story and become hopelessly identified with the characters. It's like taking a trip out of yourself. I guess it's an escape, but a pleasurable one.

For example, when Jake Sully slips into his avatar on Planet Pandora and runs into the jungle, that is such an exhilarating moment. I want to live it with him. I want to be there. I want to imagine I am him.

As a young blonde friend of mine whispered to me, while we watched James Cameron's masterpiece unfold, "I don't wanna go back to Planet Earth."

It was the same with the movie *Bohemian Rhapsody*. When Freddie Mercury seemed to have lost himself amid the seductive weirdness of the German gay scene, it didn't look like he'd make it back to London in time for the fabulous Live Aid concert in Wembley Stadium. But then, somehow, he listened to the urging of his old girlfriend Mary and decided to go for it.

The next scene was the best in the whole movie, as the camera rushed towards Wembley Stadium and then soared up and over the parapet, revealing the huge crowd inside. It was an intensely exciting and ecstatic moment, and a moment of redemption for Mercury who, with the other members of Queen backing him, became the star of the whole show.

Watching from my cinema seat, I loved the rush of that movie sequence. I was there, soaring over Wembley. I was there in the crowd, loving every moment.

So, Osho and I have to disagree on this one. Movies are the only places where I want to lose myself in someone else's fantasy and, to tell the truth, I'm a little concerned that if I become enlightened I won't be able to do that anymore. On the other hand, maybe sacrificing my movie addiction is a cheap price to pay for eternal, 24-hour bliss. We'll see.

Anyway, we have digressed into the dreamy world of Tinsel Town, whereas I was talking about the daily news and the way it's negatively slanted because that's what catches people's attention, even though it negatively affects people's state of mental health.

For example, remember when there was an outbreak of a disease called Ebola in tropical Africa? It's a particularly horrific disease because if you get it, then basically your insides turn to mush, you start bleeding internally and externally, and you have only a 50 percent chance of survival. Just to give you a comparison, with the coronavirus you have a 98 percent chance of survival.

So the media went nuts scaring people about Ebola. When scientists pointed out that Ebola has no chance of spreading in the United States, because it needs a tropical climate to survive, the media warned "Yes, but maybe it will mutate and adapt to survive here!" When the scientists explained that it is actually quite difficult to catch Ebola, the media said, "Yes, but if it becomes an airborne disease you could just catch it and die from a single sneeze!"

So, this is how it goes. This is how we grow accustomed to living in a climate of anxiety and fear. Man, I tell you, these journalists should have been around in Europe in the Middle Ages when bubonic plague was raging through country after country. The pneumonic version of the plague had a 90 percent mortality rate. You got it? You died.

What I'm suggesting is that you learn to disidentify from the news by taking a back seat and using your meditative awareness to watch yourself watching. This is a good challenge for your personal growth and one that will give you distance from the collective social mind and bring you closer and closer to yourself.

Then there's another stage: while you are watching, notice how you identify with what you think is right and what you think is wrong. This is more difficult than it sounds. For example, let's go a short way back in time and say you're watching the TV debates between Joe Biden and Donald Trump during the runup to the November election in 2020.

Now, if you think like me, then pretty soon you'll be forming a strong opinion that one of these guys is right and the other is talking through his ass — I'll leave you to guess which one got me on his side. But in the world of meditation, both men can be right, or neither man can be right, because it really doesn't matter. Whatever opinion you form will take you out of your witnessing consciousness. Why? Because you are becoming identified with what you see, and as soon as you become identified you lose your witnessing state.

Please don't misunderstand me. I'm not saying that when you become a meditator you shouldn't vote, or that you can't discriminate between two candidates and decide which one will be best at running the good old US-of-A. Of course you can. Your participation in the democratic process is a separate dimension and you're welcome to function there, as a responsible, or even as an irresponsible, citizen of society.

But there's another space, inside you, where you can experience what the Hindu seers used to say, *samsara maya hai*, the world is an illusion, and only consciousness is real. And this is where people get confused, because they start to think, *Okay, if the world is an illusion, then I won't vote for Joe Biden because it's all meaningless.* They give up on the world and withdraw to a metaphorical cave in the Himalayas, preferably with AC and shower unit built in.

This, by the way, was why Osho spent a good deal of time hammering the Indian mindset in his discourses, because, as he repeatedly said, "Only cowards try to escape from the world." Meditation and the world can walk hand in hand. If you choose one against the other you are again committing the mistake of getting identified.

But I want to get back to this habit of ours, of thinking in terms of right and wrong, because it can be so easily manipulated. In fact, every movie you have ever watched manipulates you, one way or another, without you even being aware of it.

Let's focus once more on our old friend Walt Disney and take a look at one of his big cartoon hits, *The Lion King*. Of course, Walt himself had long since departed for the "Great Disneyland in the Sky" when this animated movie was released in 1994, but his inheritors were still faithfully reproducing his formula for trivializing pretty much everything the real world has to offer.

Okay, I'm being mean to Uncle Walt, but that doesn't mean I'm not right. Anyway, I'm sure most of you know the plot of *The Lion King*, but for those who don't, here's a brief introduction:

In a wilderness region of Africa called the Pride Lands, a family of lions rules over the rest of the animal kingdom from a place called Pride Rock. Here, King Mufasa and Queen Sarabi present their newborn son, Simba, to the rest of Africa's wild animals with the understanding he will one day be king.

However, Simba has a wicked uncle called Scar who murders King Mufasa and seizes the throne, while poor Simba flees into exile. After growing up in the company of carefree outcasts, Simba returns to challenge Scar, defeats him and takes his place as the rightful king.

It's basically a four-legged rerun of Shakespeare's *Hamlet*...of course, with a happy Hollywood ending.

Now, let me begin by saying I've got nothing against lions. The first lion I ever met was in a cinema, at the beginning of a movie by Metro-Goldwyn-Mayer. His name was Leo, I enjoyed watching him roar, and as a kid I took it for granted he was the king of beasts.

But that's a myth, not a reality. If you've ever seen a herd of elephants facing down a pride of lions, you'll know what I mean. Big cats are no match for giant jumbos and for sure they themselves know it — they stay well clear of those ivory tusks and scatter when charged. Even a herd of water buffalos can trash a pride of lions when they are in an angry mood.

I'm explaining this because we get fed these social stereotypes about who gets to be king of the hill and who has to stay at the bottom. For example, at the beginning of the movie, when Simba is held up for all the other animals to admire and praise, even zebras and gazelles, who regularly get eaten by lions, are supposed to bow down and be happy.

Not only that, the hyenas are typed as the bad guys, which is so typical of our pop psychology. Since forever, hyenas have been symbolized by us human beings as mean, cowardly, cunning, and treacherous, and this movie follows the same well-trodden path.

So, in a nutshell, lions are kings, hyenas are scum, and zebras are happy to be eaten. Come on Walt, gimme a break. If I were a hyena attorney I'd sue Disney for the one billion dollars the corporation made off the film. And if I was a zebra I'd kick the crap out of Simba before he grew old enough to eat me.

And what about this king thing? As I already mentioned, King Mufasa has a nasty brother called Scar who murders him and takes over the throne. So, the audience is spoon-fed these stereotypes: Scar is the bad guy, while Mufasa is the good guy and rightful monarch. But nobody asks: who did King Mufasa murder to grab the throne in the first place?

As a parallel, take a look at human history and these so-called "royal" families that intermarry around Europe and live in fancy castles. They all come from ancestors who were robbers, killers, invaders, rapists, and thieves. Those fortune hunters slew their enemies, seized power, proclaimed themselves superior, and forced everyone else to submit to them. That's the real history of these families and so as far as I'm concerned there is no such thing as a legitimate king.

What I'm saying is: we, the audience, are being set up to admire and obey a bogus authority. We're being conned into feeling good about the guy who is on the throne and antagonistic towards the other guy, who wants to take it away from him.

As you can see, this is turning into a bit of a rant, but my point is simple: we're being manipulated into believing what's right and what's wrong. By the end of the movie, we feel perfectly okay about Simba returning from his exile in the wilderness and killing Scar in a so-called happy ending, with legitimate power restored (yes, I know, it was the hyenas who actually killed Scar, but it was Simba who threw him off the cliff).

Really, from this perspective, *The Lion King* is a re-run of those old black-and-white westerns in which the good guy shoots the bad guy in the end. The problem is: life just ain't like that. It's way more complicated.

For example, take a look at the dynamics of the 2020 presidential election; to millions of voters Donald Trump was the bad guy, Scar, whereas to millions more, he was the good guy, King Mufasa. And as we've already learned from Uncle Walt, violence is justified in the name of a just cause. Simba can kill Scar, because Scar is in the wrong.

So, when Trump announced that the election had been stolen from him, his supporters felt perfectly justified in storming the Capitol Building in an attempt to overthrow the election result. God knows what would have happened if they'd managed to get hold of House Speaker Nancy Pelosi, or any other Democrat who crossed their path.

What would Uncle Walt have said about that? Would he still have us believe that it's all part of a natural "Circle of Life" which supposedly ensures a fair and just world? Or would he have to admit that his childish cartoon morality is turning the American public into unthinking imbeciles?

However, from a meditator's point of view, no matter what is happening, right or wrong, there is always an opportunity to watch and witness. And this presents you with another interesting opportunity: to destroy the Donald Trump inside you.

It's a fascinating exercise. First, you distinguish the qualities that make Trump who he is: a feeling of self-importance, a desire to be the boss, a willingness to create "alternative facts" that support your point of view, a skewed vision of reality that allows you to feel justified in acting like a bully, ordering people around, taking over and being in charge...and so on.

Make a list of those qualities you see in him and write them down. Then, when you've done it, spend some time contemplating each of these qualities and see if you can find them inside yourself. Reflect on those times in your life when you have acted like Trump, or maybe just wanted to act like him.

In this way, you'll see how Donald Trump is a gift from the universe to help you find out this is not the way you want to live in your own life. But that doesn't mean you want go out and shoot the guy. Rather, you use him as a mirror, so you can shoot yourself – well, in a manner of speaking. Please don't take me literally. I mean, you can see the Donald Trump in you and, in the light of your awareness, allow this part of you to dissolve.

The world is always showing us something we need to discover in ourselves. The world is a fantastic teacher, because, as the supergroup USA for Africa once sang, way back in 1985, "We Are the World." It must be true because Stevie Wonder, Bob Dylan, Lionel Ritchie, and a host of superstars sang it so well.

What I'm saying is that, as Osho kept telling us, being a meditator doesn't mean that you abandon the world and retreat into self-isolation and indifference. The world needs you. You need the world. Shine the light of your awareness on it and enjoy the ride.

Chapter Sixteen

DON'T WORRY, BE HAPPY

In this world, it is very difficult to find a happy person, because nobody is fulfilling the conditions for being happy. The first condition is that one has to drop all comparison. Drop all these stupid ideas of being superior and inferior. You are neither superior nor inferior.

You are simply yourself! There exists no one like you, no one with whom you can be compared. Then, suddenly, you are at home. Osho

Creativity is a simple concept for me. It means being myself. Most people associate creativity with something really epic, such as paintings by Vincent van Gogh or a symphony by Ludwig van Beethoven. But as I see it, creativity is a simple thing: be yourself.

Live your potential; by which I mean, allow whatever is in you to find expression. And when you do this, you are creative, regardless of what it is. Cooking or cleaning your kitchen can be creative when it flows as an expression of your natural energy.

For me, creativity often comes in the moment of writing. I write about my past experiences with the clarity that I have now, looking back on them.

Just recently I saw a bumper sticker on a passing car in Amsterdam with the saying "It is never too late to have a happy childhood."

This reminded me of a quote from Osho, "Go back in the past and live your life for the first time with the tools I have given you."

This what I try to do with my writing. Naturally, I was thinking I could help the world by writing about my experience of being with Osho for 48 years. The funny thing is, after writing for a while, I discovered I was actually writing for myself.

Writing helps me get more clarity for myself. In fact, this book is a gift to myself. I feel grateful each day I am writing, since every day it turns out to be a meeting with myself. The more I write, the more I can enjoy being myself being Krishna Prem, and then I can more easily share this joy with others, and also share my crazy ideas about this whole circus of life on earth.

Somehow, I was always a writer, words danced for me. When two written words stand up and start dancing with each other, I know I am on the right track. When two words stick on the paper and cannot move, I know I have to get rid of them. It's a natural part of the process.

Even if you love your work, it is sometimes a pain, in the sense that it still sometimes needs effort, energy and motivation. But this kind of pain will soon turn into a joy. If it is the kind of pain that leads to more pain, then it's probably a sign you are trying too hard at something that does not really suit you.

I remember people coming to ask questions of Osho and one of the first things they'd say is how unhappy they felt about their jobs. For example, there were doctors or lawyers who in their youth wanted to be musicians or artists, but then they'd invested so many years in professional training that they gave up on their dreams and followed the path of least resistance. And, of course, money and security had something to do with it — you can't beat a regular monthly salary, right?

When you confess these kinds of things to a mystic, if he's the real deal, he will encourage you to follow your heart. It will be more risky, of course, but, come to think of it, not as risky as getting involved with your mystic! I always had the feeling that Osho would encourage people to take any kind of risks in their lives because he already knew that meeting him was the greatest risk anyone could take.

So, creativity means finding one's own song and allowing it to be expressed. In effect, to sing it. This also means you are starting to trust yourself, starting to gather courage to follow your heart. But you need to be careful here because the conventional mythology of the American Dream sounds similar, but it's very different.

The American Dream says that anyone can do anything. All you have to do is go for it, try harder, make it happen...and one day, boom, there it is. But as Peggy Lee once sang about the "things that you're liable to read in the Bible," it ain't necessarily so. Not everyone can be a millionaire, play in the Superbowl, travel to the moon, or become President of the United States.

So, what do I mean, when I say have the courage to follow your heart? I mean, set aside the fantasies that have been fed into your mind by our mass culture, and set aside your fears of survival, and listen to your own energy. What does it want to do? How does it want to express itself? What turns you on?

Once you know, then you can start taking baby steps in that direction and my advice is: be sure to enjoy the journey as you go, because there's no certainty you will reach your goal. You may love your singing lessons, which is great, but that doesn't mean you're going to win an all-American talent contest.

Osho was an enormous help for me to become myself. I remember I was once sitting in the meditation hall in Pune, listening to him give a discourse in Hindi. I didn't understand a word, but I could appreciate being there, because he was speaking in a very melodic, poetic manner and that was kinda relaxing and peaceful.

So, I just went along with the flow of sound, maybe dozing off a little bit, when suddenly, out of nowhere, in the middle of a 90-minute lecture, he said one sentence in English, "Life is a bridge, walk over it, but build no house on it."

This sentence was exactly the message I needed to hear, even though I couldn't understand anything else from the talk. At first, it came to me in the form of an intellectual understanding, but soon it sank deeper and one day it really helped me.

Not long afterwards, I found myself becoming incredibly emotional when a woman whom I dearly loved decided to leave me for another guy. Frankly, I wanted to die. I was getting completely tangled up and identified with my emotions and could see no light at the end of the tunnel. But as the turmoil slowly subsided, I remembered what Osho had said that day in discourse and began to understand that feelings come and go. Even the most powerful, intense emotions rise up, swamp you and then fade away. Sometimes in life you are happy, sometimes sad.

By the way, some of you will recognize the quote. Osho was referring to a saying, attributed to Jesus, which an Indian emperor carved in stone on a bridge leading into a fabulous city. He built the city, intending to move his capital there, but in the end it was never lived in. The emperor lost interest and for some reason there was no water supply available, so the city died before it was hardly born. It's still there, in the desert. It's called Fatehpur Sikri.

To me, feelings are like a bridge on which you should not build your house. They come and they go. One day they seem so solid and have eternal foundations, next day the feelings shift and something else is happening. That's life. The trick is to find your center, so you can watch these tidal waves of emotion wash over you and remain a witness to it all.

In this book, I include Osho quotes that resonate with me, that help me remember the deeper truth of what my teacher was saying: "I use words to indicate silence. When I speak, it is not what I say, it is how you receive it, how you relax with it."

For me, silence comes first. I don't think it's the case just for me and for Osho, but for everything, for the whole existence. Silence is primordial, eternal, unborn and forever. My Christian friends like to quote the beginning of Genesis: "In the beginning was the Word...." But this doesn't make a whole lot of sense to me. If somebody asks me to rewrite Genesis I would say: "In the beginning was silence and out of that silence emerged the sounds of life...." When all the sounds of life have been lived, then in death we again return to silence.

When we are in meditation we are as close as we can get to silence, and the marketplace is at the opposite polarity, at the other end of the spectrum, where all the noise is to be found, but that doesn't make the marketplace a bad place to be.

Think about the left side of an infinity sign as meditation and the right side as the marketplace. Together, they allow us to remember that we come from silence and return to silence, but unless they include each other, unless we include meditation in the marketplace, we will never know what life is about.

I am looking at the big picture now, seeing how we came from silence and we return to silence, and in between these two quiet moments, we experience the amazing sounds of life, and we need to celebrate them as much as possible.

I have been around many people who were dying. In their last moments, I was fortunate enough to be with them. I couldn't believe how beautiful these people became just before they died. I couldn't believe how much they were capable of returning to love on their way to disappearing into silence.

I am not talking about especially meditative people. I'm not referring to people who were so spiritual they could be said to be almost enlightened and capable of watching their own death as it happened to them, although I'm told by the mystics it can be done. No, I'm not talking about any advanced beings here.

I am talking about ordinary people like you and me. They would become love just before they died and I could just about hear the whisper of their voices; I could just about hear them say, "Krishna Prem, I love you."

I was deeply touched, very impressed by the awesomeness of regular people. And it gives a purpose to this book, in my eyes, because we come from silence and we return to silence, and between the two we have an opportunity to experience love and share it with others. That's what I'm doing now.

We come from silence, we return to silence, but as you may have noticed there is a long time in between those two moments – sometimes 70, 80, 90 years – and even though people want to live as long as possible they mostly don't really have a purpose for doing so.

If I ask you, "Do you want to live till you are 90?" you will say yes, but if I ask "For what?" do you have something more to say? Most people are afraid of death, so they want to live longer in order to postpone it, and this becomes the reason to continue.

I can totally relate to that. On one occasion I came close to death myself and I didn't want to go the rest of the way. It happened in a swimming pool while I was doing a meditation called Total Immersion Swimming. It's a beautiful experience – you swim like a fish, you take a breath every six strokes and you just glide through the water.

It was developed by a Russian guy named Alexander Popov who was winning Olympic medals without showing any signs of exhaustion at the end of a race, without even breathing heavily. He was a meditative swimmer but the Americans couldn't tolerate it because the USA was accustomed to grabbing a big haul of swimming medals at every Olympic Games, whereas now Popov was taking some of them instead.

So, they studied him scientifically and that's why these days many of us are swimming like Popov. I personally am not winning so many gold medals, but it is a beautiful way to glide through the pool while meditating.

One day, while swimming, I started to feel that my body was not well, but I didn't take it seriously. I was laughing and thinking to myself, *What's wrong with me? What's wrong with my tempo right now?* I got out of the water, showered and got ready for the evening meditation, which lasted about two hours.

Afterwards, there was a dance party and I met a woman on the dance floor and later we went to my room. I remember she asked me, "Do you want to die?" I swear, I thought she was offering to make love with me so beautifully, so orgasmically, that I would think I'd died and gone to heaven. Some people say I've got a one-track mind...but that's another story.

This woman was stunning, I was attracted to her but while we'd been dancing together I didn't get the impression she was so attracted to me. So, I was pleasantly surprised when she insisted on walking me up to my room.

When we got there, she asked me "Do you want to die?" and I got excited. Of course, I went over to try to kiss her but got a real shock when she slapped my face and said, "I'm not talking about making love! I'm talking about you! You don't look healthy to me. I'm asking you whether you want to die tonight!"

I was confused and said, "I don't know what you're talking about." I didn't feel well but, like they say, denial is not the name of a river in Egypt. I wasn't so much in touch with what was going on in my body, whereas she could see it was serious.

So, she went back to the dance floor to fetch the guy who'd been dancing beside us, who happened to be a doctor. He took one look at me and said, "Let's go to the hospital." It seemed like no big deal at the time, but these are the two people who saved my life: the woman who didn't want sex with me and the doctor who just happened to be dancing next to us.

At the hospital they said, "We need to check your heart. We think it is indigestion, but we need to check your heart first. How do you feel about that?"

I said, "Well, if you and this doctor friend of mine agree, let's do it."

So, I lay down on a stretcher and they shot me up with an anesthetic that felt absolutely fabulous. I hadn't done drugs in years and I was really impressed with this medication. I was super-stoned, totally relaxed, and had no idea what was happening and what these doctors were doing.

Sometime later, I was lying in a hospital bed and a couple of doctors came and said, "We're happy to tell you the operation was successful."

I was puzzled and asked, "What operation are you talking about?"

And they said, "Well, you just had a heart attack and we needed to put in two stents to keep your blood vessels open and functioning properly."

My first thought was, *My gosh, how could a meditator have a heart attack?* I had fallen for the assumption that meditation would always take care of my physical body and the temple housing my consciousness would never die. This was a rude awakening, a very rude awakening.

Afterwards, I reflected on how easily I cruised through the whole thing, because I didn't know what was happening to me. If the doctors had told me I was having a heart attack, I don't know if I would have been such a model patient. Maybe I would have freaked out, not acting so calm and easygoing. I was a hero by accident, not knowing the danger.

I feel great now. I'm back to thinking that I'm going to live forever, which by the time you read this book may not be true — you never know. But it is interesting how I learned that meditation is no guarantee against a heart attack. And it is no guarantee that you will not leave your body one day. This book is about dancing, not about living forever. It is about enjoying the time while you are here.

When I later saw that girl, of course, I had to thank her. She laughed. She didn't hit me this time, but I didn't try to kiss her either. I learned my lesson. She saved my life by walking me to my room. I thought she was coming to bed but she was actually coming to see if I was dying — I reckon that's a pretty cool story.

And, by the way, I'd certainly like to get my hands on some of that medication again – but, on reflection, it's not worth having another heart attack just to get stoned.

So, this book is not about living forever, it is about living well while you are here.

Anytime you almost die, like I did, it is a humbling experience and I think that's why people find it easy to become so loving when they are just about to die. In the face of death, they become humble human beings, and in that state of humbleness it's easy and natural for them to slip into their hearts and realize that love is the most important thing about being alive.

It doesn't happen to everyone. Some people still want to go on running the world after they've died, so they make out a very detailed will about what should happen next. A friend of mine was like that. She made a list of people who she wanted at her death celebration, after the funeral, and she even explained what kind of cake she wanted for people to eat.

That was kinda cute. One of her long-term boyfriends was a good baker and he could make this special layer cake, filled with cream and jam and custard...just delicious. But she didn't like that cake. She loved him but she hated the cake. So, in her will, she said "He is not to make that cake for my party!" I loved it. And she did die well and peacefully.

Speaking of humbleness, I sometimes wonder about this idea of Papal Infallibility. There is a pope in me, just as there is a pope in you, who thinks he's got the whole spiritual thing nailed down, who thinks he knows better than everyone else, and cannot make a mistake. But there's also an official Pope in the Vatican who has the power to make infallible announcements. When he does so, 1.2 billion Catholics think he can't make a mistake because he is the official representative of JC and his dad — or so the doctrine of infallibility goes.

But I wonder: when the Pope goes into his room, as soon as he is alone, does he throw up his hands up and say, *Who me? Infallible? I can make a mistake every day!*

Alone in his room, he knows how fallible he is. It does not make him less of a man. In fact, in my view, it makes him a great man because he has a chance to say to JC, "I am humbled by this job and I am going to do the best I can." This for me, is a sign of greatness.

It's not easy to be a great Pope but it is possible. It is not easy to be a great president of the United States, but it is possible. Which reminds me, in America, we always say to our children, "You could be the next President of the United States."

But the fact is there is only one president every four years, or one president every eight years, and we have millions of kids in this country. So, I think this is a terrible thing to tell children, that one day they could be a president.

Why not say, "One day you can be a unique person?" Or maybe, "You are already a unique, special person. You don't have to become anyone else. You just have to find out who you are. Life is an adventure of self-discovery."

Why do we plant this kind of ambition in or children? Instead of saying to them, you can be a president for four years, why don't we say: you can be your own person for life? That is more true, because everyone is born to be themselves.

This book, as you have gathered, is about being yourself and loving yourself. We need to get out of the crowd, then we need to get the crowd out of us, so we can love ourselves and enjoy life in a natural way. We need to free ourselves from all those voices of our relatives, who, with the best of intentions, tried to shape us in their own image.

This reminds me of a young woman who left Brazil to seek the meaning of her life. It's a neat story, reflecting something that can happen to all of us, one way or another, so maybe this is a good way to bring this book to an end.

Let's call this woman Maria, because Brazil is a Catholic country and so many little girls are given the name of JC's mother. Well, Maria left Brazil to travel the world and ended up in an ashram in India. I was in a therapy group with her, where we were invited to look at the way we'd been treated by our family members when we were little.

Maria was very upset because her grandfather had physically abused her. He would hit her constantly and say, "You are wrong!" In this therapy group, she stopped being that frightened, helpless little girl. She realized that she wasn't wrong, she was just scared to be herself because every time she tried to be that, she would get a slap from her grandfather.

She returned to Brazil as a self-confident woman and a disciple of Osho, wearing orange clothes and a necklace of wooden beads with a picture of her teacher hanging from it in a locket.

Her grandfather, of course, was a staunch Catholic, so when he saw her walk in the door he came over to hit her again. But this time she was ready. This time, too, she was strong, not only physically but also psychologically. She caught his hand, stopped him and said, "Never hit me again. Never."

She became enlightened, just there, standing up to her grandfather. And he never did try to hit her again, by the way.

So maybe, as we come to the end of this book, you need to ask yourself, *How many people have tried to tell me who I am?* It does not have to be a violent grandfather, it could be a grandfather who loves you, but who doesn't trust life enough to give you the gift called, "Find out for yourself."

To me, life is the big picture. The big picture is called meditation, and by meditation I mean learning the knack of discovering the witnessing consciousness inside you. Meditation is the art of discovering you are already the big picture, that you are existence itself.

Now, I have a confession to make: the truth is that you will end this book not knowing anything at all. I am sorry to tell you this, now, at the end, but if I'd done so at the beginning you probably wouldn't have been willing to buy my book in the first place.

But, hey, if not knowing anything helps you dance, helps you sing, puts you in a good mood and helps you celebrate, this is a good book. Because later on, maybe when you are swimming in a pool and you have a heart attack, you might say, *I am not here forever, I need to learn to meditate.*

Celebration and meditation go hand in hand. This book is encouraging you to meditate from this moment on, whether you are 15 years old or 50 years old, and to celebrate your life for no particular reason, simply out of the joy of being yourself.

That's about it. Here we are at the end of my book and, as they say in my home country, "Be sure to have a nice day." See you on the dance floor, or in the swimming pool, okay?

(continued from front page)
Or you can leave your personality shattered on the ground and trust your buddha nature. As a buddha, you will thank your parents for making love, as you are so thankful that you are alive right now.

You may still have conditioning, but it will be more like clothing that you can put on and take off. Now your conditioning will not be you.

You can't do this without falling in love with yourself. And in order to become a new man, a new woman, you must encounter your aloneness.

Aloneness is a love story. Only when you learn to be alone without being lonely can you meet yourself and others in meditation and delight.

Aloneness, a love story, is a journey from birth to death. Yes you are a human being. You are also a buddha. Wake up and enjoy. Only when you and the buddha are one, you have come home.

Love is,
Krishna Prem

Krishna Prem *is the author of the book Gee You Are You, available on Amazon. He lives 6 months a year in Pune, India, at the OSHO International Meditation Resort and 6 months a year he travels in Europe, America, and Asia, leading weekend Meditation Retreats. Details are included on his website www.geeyouareyou.com.*

KP, as he is often called, is also well versed in Advaita Meditation. His teaching includes that "We are one existence appearing as two friends."

Printed in Poland
by Amazon Fulfillment
Poland Sp. z o.o., Wrocław